Math Practice: Grades 3–4

Table of Contents

Addition

Addition with Numbers Through 9....................................4
Two-Digit Addition 6
Two-Digit Column Addition...7
Three-Digit Addition with Regrouping............................8
Two-, Three-, and Four-Digit Column Addition
   with Regrouping 10
Three- and Four-Digit Column Addition
   with Regrouping 11
Four-Digit Addition with Regrouping 12
Addition of Decimals.. 14
Addition of Fractions 18

Subtraction

Subtraction with Numbers Through 12....................... 20
Subtraction with Numbers Through 18....................... 21
Subtraction with Numbers Through 19....................... 22
Two-Digit Subtraction.. 24
Two-Digit Subtraction with Regrouping...................... 25
Two- and Three-Digit Subtraction
   with Regrouping 26
Three-Digit Subtraction with Regrouping................... 27
Three- and Four-Digit Subtraction
   with Regrouping 29
Four-Digit Subtraction with Regrouping 30
Four-Digit Subtraction.. 31
Five-Digit Subtraction... 32
Subtraction of Decimals... 33
Subtraction of Fractions... 35

Multiplication

Multiplication with the Factor 2 36
Multiplication with Factors 0–2 37
Multiplication with the Factor 3 38
Multiplication with Factors 2 and 3 39
Multiplication with the Factor 4 40
Multiplication with Factors 2–4 41
Multiplication with the Factor 5 42
Multiplication with Factors 4 and 5 43
Multiplication with Factors 2–5 44
Multiplication with the Factor 6 45
Multiplication with the Factor 7 46

Multiplication with Fa.. 7
Multiplication with the Factor 8 48
Multiplication with the Factor 9 49
Multiplication with Factors 8 and 9 50
Multiplication with Factors 6–9 51
Multiplication with Factors 2–9 52
Multiplication with Factors 8–10 56
Multiplication with Factors 11 and 12........................ 57
Two-Digit by One-Digit Multiplication 58
Two-Digit by One-Digit Multiplication
   with Regrouping 59
Three-Digit by One-Digit Multiplication
   with Regrouping 65
Three-Digit by One-Digit Multiplication 66
Four-Digit by One-Digit Multiplication
   with Regrouping 67
Two-Digit by Two-Digit Multiplication
   with Regrouping 69
Three-Digit by Two-Digit Multiplication
   with Regrouping 71
Three-Digit by Three-Digit Multiplication
   with Regrouping 73
Multiplication of Decimals...74

Division

Division with One-Digit Quotients.............................. 78
Division with One-Digit Quotients
   and Remainders 84
Division with Two-Digit Quotients.............................. 89
Division with Two-Digit Quotients
   and Remainders 92
Division with Two- and Three-Digit Quotients 97
Division with Three-Digit Quotients
   and Remainders 98
Division with Two- and Three-Digit Quotients
   and Remainders 99
Division with Four-Digit Dividends 101
Division with Two-Digit Divisors
   and Remainders 102

Answer Key..104

ISBN 978-1-60418-270-5

03-265121151

Ready-to-Use Ideas and Activities

The only way that students will truly be able to manipulate numbers and have access to higher-level math concepts is to learn the basic facts and understand fundamental concepts, such as counting, addition, subtraction, multiplication, and division.

The following activities can help reinforce basic skills. These activities include a multisensory approach to helping students understand the concepts being introduced.

- Place a container filled with plastic discs near students' workspace. Plastic discs make great counters, which are extremely beneficial in helping students visualize mathematical concepts.

- Separate the flash cards provided in the back of this book. Start with a flash card that shows small numbers, and put it on a flat surface. Then, use the discs to show what is on the flash card. For example, to show 8 × 3 = 24, lay out 3 groups of 8 discs each. Explain that when you make 3 groups of 8 discs, you have 24 discs total.

- After doing a number of examples using the flash cards, let students use the discs to make their own problems and show them visually.

CD-104320 • © Carson-Dellosa

Ready-to-Use Ideas and Activities

- Use a pair of dice and anything that can act as a three-minute timer (a timer, a stopwatch, a watch with a second hand, etc.), or decide on a certain number of rounds of play. Have each student roll the dice and add the numbers on the top faces. Each correct answer is worth one point. The student with the most correct answers after a specific period of time or number of rounds wins. For example, a game may consist of six rounds. The student with the most points after six rounds wins. Alternately, the game can be played with subtraction, multiplication, or division with remainders.

- As players memorize answers and gain confidence, add additional dice. When using more than two dice, have players state the problem aloud and answer as they go. For example, if the dice show 3, 6, and 4, the player would say, "3 plus 6 is 9 and 9 plus 4 is 13."

- Create a bingo sheet with five rows and five columns of blank squares. Write *FREE* in the middle square. Give one cupy to each student. Write the flash card problems where students can see them and have students choose 24 problems to write in the empty spaces of their bingo cards.

- When students have finished filling out their bingo cards, make the flash cards into a deck. Call out the answers one at a time. If a student has a problem on his card that equals the called-out answer, he should draw an X through the problem to cross it out. Allow only one problem per answer. The student who crosses out five problems in a row first (horizontally, vertically, or diagonally) wins the game by calling, "Bingo!"

- Play another version of this game by writing answers on the bingo sheet and calling out the problems. To extend the game, continue playing until a student crosses out all of the problems on her bingo sheet.

Addition with Numbers Through 9

Solve each problem.

Step Up to the Plate!

1.   4
  + 8

2.   3
  + 2

3.   8
  + 3

4.   7
  + 3

5.   3
  + 3

6.   2
  + 2

7.   7
  + 4

8.   2
  + 1

9.   4
  + 0

10.   5
  + 2

11.   4
  + 9

12.   2
  + 9

13.   3
  + 0

14.   6
  + 2

15.   4
  + 4

16.   1
  + 2

17.   4
  + 6

18.   4
  + 3

19.   5
  + 4

20.   4
  + 2

21.   1
  + 3

22.   4
  + 6

23.   8
  + 2

24.   2
  + 5

25.   2
  + 7

26.   2
  + 3

27.   3
  + 5

28.   9
  + 3

29.   3
  + 7

30.   3
  + 4

31.   2
  + 4

32.   6
  + 3

33.   2
  + 0

Name _____   Date _____

Addition with Numbers Through 9

Total Problems: **33**
Problems Correct: _____

Solve each problem.

Practice Makes Perfect!

1. $\begin{array}{r} 7 \\ +6 \\ \hline \end{array}$
2. $\begin{array}{r} 7 \\ +7 \\ \hline \end{array}$
3. $\begin{array}{r} 3 \\ +6 \\ \hline \end{array}$
4. $\begin{array}{r} 4 \\ +3 \\ \hline \end{array}$
5. $\begin{array}{r} 7 \\ +4 \\ \hline \end{array}$
6. $\begin{array}{r} 5 \\ +4 \\ \hline \end{array}$

7. $\begin{array}{r} 6 \\ +5 \\ \hline \end{array}$
8. $\begin{array}{r} 9 \\ +8 \\ \hline \end{array}$
9. $\begin{array}{r} 8 \\ +4 \\ \hline \end{array}$
10. $\begin{array}{r} 6 \\ +2 \\ \hline \end{array}$
11. $\begin{array}{r} 3 \\ +2 \\ \hline \end{array}$
12. $\begin{array}{r} 3 \\ +9 \\ \hline \end{array}$

13. $\begin{array}{r} 3 \\ +3 \\ \hline \end{array}$
14. $\begin{array}{r} 9 \\ +5 \\ \hline \end{array}$
15. $\begin{array}{r} 9 \\ +6 \\ \hline \end{array}$
16. $\begin{array}{r} 2 \\ +7 \\ \hline \end{array}$
17. $\begin{array}{r} 6 \\ +4 \\ \hline \end{array}$
18. $\begin{array}{r} 5 \\ +8 \\ \hline \end{array}$

19. $\begin{array}{r} 3 \\ +7 \\ \hline \end{array}$
20. $\begin{array}{r} 6 \\ +8 \\ \hline \end{array}$
21. $\begin{array}{r} 8 \\ +3 \\ \hline \end{array}$
22. $\begin{array}{r} 5 \\ +4 \\ \hline \end{array}$
23. $\begin{array}{r} 9 \\ +1 \\ \hline \end{array}$
24. $\begin{array}{r} 9 \\ +8 \\ \hline \end{array}$

25. $\begin{array}{r} 2 \\ +3 \\ \hline \end{array}$
26. $\begin{array}{r} 3 \\ +5 \\ \hline \end{array}$
27. $\begin{array}{r} 8 \\ +9 \\ \hline \end{array}$
28. $\begin{array}{r} 4 \\ +3 \\ \hline \end{array}$
29. $\begin{array}{r} 8 \\ +8 \\ \hline \end{array}$
30. $\begin{array}{r} 3 \\ +3 \\ \hline \end{array}$

31. $\begin{array}{r} 9 \\ +7 \\ \hline \end{array}$
32. $\begin{array}{r} 8 \\ +7 \\ \hline \end{array}$
33. $\begin{array}{r} 7 \\ +3 \\ \hline \end{array}$

Two-Digit Addition

Solve each problem. Regroup when necessary.

A Good Attitude Is the Key!

1. 55
  + 84

2. 39
  + 97

3. 65
  + 47

4. 44
  + 25

5. 84
  + 14

6. 68
  + 75

7. 58
  + 26

8. 64
  + 56

9. 87
  + 13

10. 61
  + 27

11. 74
  + 33

12. 78
  + 15

13. 25
  + 89

14. 65
  + 22

15. 34
  + 52

16. 89
  + 53

17. 87
  + 46

18. 47
  + 56

19. 69
  + 33

20. 27
  + 42

21. 87
  + 45

22. 56
  + 35

23. 95
  + 68

24. 36
  + 27

25. 37
  + 45

26. 56
  + 33

27. 67
  + 40

28. 24
  + 78

29. 64
  + 85

30. 29
  + 45

31. 73
  + 26

32. 74
  + 25

33. 49
  + 37

CD-104320 • © Carson-Dellosa

Two-Digit Column Addition

Total Problems: **22**
Problems Correct: _____

Solve each problem. Regroup when necessary.

Unlock the Secrets of Addition!

1. 24 41 + 32	**2.** 91 28 + 13	**3.** 35 66 + 37	**4.** 22 61 + 84	**5.** 16 10 + 31	**6.** 45 32 + 48
7. 45 52 + 21	**8.** 28 39 + 21	**9.** 27 65 + 85	**10.** 74 26 + 39	**11.** 55 21 + 37	**12.** 33 30 + 36
13. 57 42 + 33	**14.** 38 46 + 23	**15.** 17 36 + 22	**16.** 85 36 + 74	**17.** 76 23 + 67	**18.** 56 21 + 32
19. 39 48 + 59	**20.** 45 23 + 54	**21.** 24 51 + 76	**22.** 25 45 + 56		

Three-Digit Addition with Regrouping

Solve each problem. Regroup when necessary.

Math Is a Gift!

1. 634
     + 268

2. 987
     + 489

3. 493
     + 277

4. 888
     + 277

5. 732
     + 299

6. 276
     + 947

7. 394
     + 496

8. 557
     + 323

9. 254
     + 347

10. 665
      + 337

11. 493
      + 229

12. 988
      + 748

13. 376
      + 266

14. 349
      + 233

15. 878
      + 287

16. 436
      + 296

17. 348
      + 948

18. 498
      + 439

19. 477
      + 298

20. 396
      + 474

21. 901
      + 109

22. 834
      + 249

23. 499
      + 292

24. 118
      + 953

25. 549
      + 202

26. 653
      + 307

27. 476
      + 498

Three-Digit Addition with Regrouping

Total Problems: **33**
Problems Correct: _____

Solve each problem. Regroup when necessary.

Get Wrapped Up in Addition!

1. 566
+ 467

2. 979
+ 354

3. 945
+ 379

4. 888
+ 276

5. 871
+ 739

6. 478
+ 655

7. 675
+ 597

8. 456
+ 327

9. 254
+ 347

10. 349
+ 493

11. 765
+ 428

12. 834
+ 666

13. 238
+ 348

14. 349
+ 233

15. 434
+ 948

16. 869
+ 572

17. 458
+ 749

18. 638
+ 422

19. 539
+ 468

20. 396
+ 578

21. 955
+ 134

22. 367
+ 984

23. 588
+ 294

24. 493
+ 327

25. 669
+ 291

26. 455
+ 347

27. 646
+ 668

28. 877
+ 353

29. 123
+ 238

30. 348
+ 489

31. 239
+ 593

32. 159
+ 485

33. 648
+ 437

Two-, Three-, and Four-Digit Column Addition with Regrouping

Solve each problem. Regroup when necessary.

You're a Winner!

1. 3,878
    4,981
  + 8,165

2. 9,651
    3,321
  + 2,283

3. 3,981
    2,357
  + 4,652

4. 76
    59
  + 53

5. 34
    67
  + 24

6. 776
    453
  + 719

7. 5,349
    3,274
  + 7,184

8. 676
    734
  + 651

9. 7,028
    4,354
  + 5,684

10. 6,048
    3,278
  + 5,328

11. 4,348
    3,451
  + 2,734

12. 343
    608
  + 789

13. 4,340
    5,433
  + 3,238

14. 356
    674
  + 380

15. 54
    39
  + 73

16. 634
    198
  + 518

17. 67
    98
  + 74

18. 5,367
    3,190
  + 1,499

19. 47
    34
  + 99

20. 321
    436
  + 548

21. 2,783
    2,546
  + 6,748

22. 9,418
    8,009
  + 7,245

   CD-104320 • © Carson-Dellosa

Three- and Four-Digit Column Addition with Regrouping

Solve each problem. Regroup when necessary.

Go for the Gold!

1.	378	2.	6,382	3.	435	4.	526	5.	528	6.	652
	943		7,452		526		452		754		751
	+ 549		+ 6,789		+ 268		+ 498		+ 294		+ 439

7.	3,658	8.	457	9.	7,458	10.	6,356	11.	8,236	12.	5,256
	2,814		989		4,349		5,093		5,548		8,248
	+ 3,856		+ 276		+ 5,962		+ 3,637		+ 5,327		+ 4,241

13.	6,898	14.	8,459	15.	525	16.	5,265	17.	2,147	18.	654
	5,433		4,908		653		2,278		3,255		452
	+ 2,154		+ 4,356		+ 896		+ 8,365		+ 2,256		+ 138

19.	7,092	20.	5,768	21.	4,265	22.	8,214
	5,405		6,937		5,124		7,716
	+ 6,124		+ 7,034		+ 6,489		+ 6,389

Four-Digit Addition with Regrouping

Solve each problem. Regroup when necessary.

Fly High with Math!

1. 4,936
   + 5,432

2. 9,675
   + 4,283

3. 5,349
   + 6,393

4. 6,434
   + 6,398

5. 9,231
   + 5,332

6. 7,221
   + 2,418

7. 6,376
   + 2,019

8. 2,393
   + 4,392

9. 8,293
   + 4,239

10. 3,768
    + 5,949

11. 1,665
    + 3,773

12. 2,343
    + 7,328

13. 7,320
    + 5,394

14. 9,347
    + 7,323

15. 8,659
    + 9,347

16. 3,424
    + 9,483

17. 6,784
    + 1,296

18. 4,392
    + 4,959

19. 1,749
    + 2,323

20. 8,459
    + 4,398

21. 6,437
    + 7,219

22. 3,829
    + 2,933

23. 5,845
    + 2,568

24. 3,490
    + 6,349

25. 5,344
    + 6,349

26. 3,282
    + 5,342

27. 5,349
    + 8,563

28. 4,372
    + 7,839

29. 7,841
    + 6,760

30. 2,404
    + 8,403

31. 3,203
    + 5,893

32. 8,349
    + 7,346

33. 8,453
    + 4,267

Four-Digit Addition with Regrouping

Solve each problem. Regroup when necessary.

Up, Up, Up and Away with Addition!

1. 3,878
  + 8,456

2. 9,675
  + 4,283

3. 3,534
  + 4,652

4. 8,900
  + 3,957

5. 9,231
  + 5,332

6. 8,569
  + 2,546

7. 6,376
  + 2,019

8. 5,349
  + 7,345

9. 4,324
  + 5,769

10. 6,909
  + 3,212

11. 7,458
  + 5,494

12. 2,343
  + 7,328

13. 4,348
  + 2,734

14. 5,343
  + 8,223

15. 8,999
  + 3,856

16. 4,340
  + 3,264

17. 8,456
  + 4,380

18. 4,392
  + 4,959

19. 3,234
  + 2,923

20. 4,348
  + 9,574

21. 7,090
  + 5,845

22. 5,345
  + 1,433

23. 3,287
  + 5,122

24. 3,490
  + 6,349

25. 4,346
  + 6,333

26. 9,895
  + 7,459

27. 7,989
  + 5,915

28. 3,259
  + 6,323

29. 6,381
  + 6,743

30. 2,404
  + 8,654

31. 4,646
  + 3,984

32. 5,913
  + 2,264

33. 8,964
  + 1,651

Addition of Decimals

Solve each problem. Regroup when necessary.

Keep Your Focus!

1. 6.34
    + 2.68

2. 9.87
    + 4.89

3. 4.93
    + 2.77

4. 8.88
    + 2.76

5. 7.32
    + 2.99

6. 2.76
    + 9.47

7. 3.94
    + 4.96

8. 5.57
    + 3.23

9. 2.54
    + 3.47

10. 6.65
    + 3.37

11. 4.93
    + 2.29

12. 9.88
    + 7.48

13. 3.76
    + 2.66

14. 3.49
    + 2.33

15. 8.78
    + 2.87

16. 4.36
    + 2.96

17. 3.48
    + 9.48

18. 4.98
    + 4.39

19. 4.77
    + 2.98

20. 3.96
    + 4.74

21. 9.01
    + 1.09

22. 8.34
    + 2.49

23. 4.99
    + 2.92

24. 1.18
    + 9.53

25. 5.49
    + 2.02

26. 6.53
    + 3.07

27. 4.76
    + 4.98

28. 9.45
    + 3.68

29. 1.13
    + 2.98

30. 3.93
    + 2.98

31. 2.36
    + 5.87

32. 2.57
    + 5.86

33. 5.47
    + 2.49

Addition of Decimals

Solve each problem. Regroup when necessary.

Zooming Through Addition!

1. 5.66 + 4.67	**2.** 9.79 + 3.54	**3.** 9.45 + 3.79	**4.** 8.88 + 2.76	**5.** 8.70 + 7.39	**6.** 4.78 + 6.55
7. 6.75 + 5.97	**8.** 4.56 + 3.27	**9.** 2.54 + 3.47	**10.** 3.49 + 4.93	**11.** 7.65 + 4.28	**12.** 8.34 + 6.65
13. 2.38 + 3.48	**14.** 3.49 + 2.33	**15.** 4.34 + 9.48	**16.** 8.69 + 5.72	**17.** 4.58 + 7.49	**18.** 6.38 + 4.22
19. 5.39 + 4.68	**20.** 3.96 + 5.78	**21.** 9.55 + 1.34	**22.** 3.67 + 9.84	**23.** 5.88 + 2.94	**24.** 4.93 + 3.27
25. 6.46 + 2.91	**26.** 4.55 + 3.47	**27.** 6.46 + 6.68	**28.** 8.77 + 3.52	**29.** 1.23 + 2.38	**30.** 3.48 + 4.89
31. 2.39 + 5.93	**32.** 1.59 + 4.85	**33.** 6.48 + 4.37			

Addition of Decimals

Solve each problem. Regroup when necessary.

Total Problems: **33**
Problems Correct: _____

You're Doing It!

1. 49.36 $+\ 54.32$	**2.** 96.75 $+\ 42.83$	**3.** 53.49 $+\ 63.93$	**4.** 64.34 $+\ 63.98$	**5.** 92.31 $+\ 53.32$	**6.** 72.21 $+\ 24.18$

7. 63.76 $+\ 20.19$	**8.** 23.93 $+\ 43.68$	**9.** 82.93 $+\ 42.18$	**10.** 37.68 $+\ 59.37$	**11.** 16.65 $+\ 37.73$	**12.** 23.43 $+\ 73.28$

13. 73.20 $+\ 53.94$	**14.** 93.47 $+\ 73.23$	**15.** 86.59 $+\ 93.47$	**16.** 34.24 $+\ 94.83$	**17.** 67.84 $+\ 12.96$	**18.** 43.92 $+\ 49.28$

19. 17.49 $+\ 23.23$	**20.** 84.77 $+\ 43.12$	**21.** 64.37 $+\ 72.19$	**22.** 38.29 $+\ 29.33$	**23.** 58.45 $+\ 25.68$	**24.** 34.90 $+\ 63.49$

25. 53.44 $+\ 67.90$	**26.** 32.02 $+\ 53.78$	**27.** 53.49 $+\ 85.63$	**28.** 43.72 $+\ 78.39$	**29.** 78.41 $+\ 67.60$	**30.** 24.04 $+\ 84.03$

31. 32.03 $+\ 53.68$	**32.** 84.53 $+\ 42.67$	**33.** 83.18 $+\ 73.46$

Name _____ Date _____

Addition of Decimals

Total Problems: **33**
Problems Correct: _____

Solve each problem. Regroup when necessary.

You're a Success!

1. 38.78
  + 84.56

2. 96.75
  + 42.83

3. 32.34
  + 46.52

4. 89.00
  + 39.57

5. 92.31
  + 53.32

6. 85.69
  + 25.46

7. 63.76
  + 20.19

8. 53.49
  + 73.45

9. 43.24
  + 57.69

10. 69.09
  + 32.12

11. 74.58
  + 54.94

12. 23.43
  + 73.28

13. 43.48
  + 27.34

14. 53.43
  + 82.23

15. 89.99
  + 38.56

16. 43.40
  + 32.34

17. 84.56
  + 43.80

18. 43.92
  + 49.59

19. 32.34
  + 23.23

20. 43.48
  + 95.74

21. 70.90
  + 58.45

22. 53.45
  + 14.35

23. 32.87
  + 51.22

24. 34.90
  + 63.49

25. 43.46
  + 63.33

26. 98.95
  + 74.59

27. 79.89
  + 59.15

28. 32.59
  + 63.23

29. 63.81
  + 37.43

30. 24.04
  + 84.03

31. 43.84
  + 32.51

32. 52.38
  + 28.41

33. 83.45
  + 14.89

Addition of Fractions

Total Problems: **15**
Problems Correct: _____

Solve each problem. Write the answer in its simplest form.

Let's Go for a Ride!

1. $\frac{1}{3} + \frac{2}{3} =$ **2.** $\frac{2}{9} + \frac{5}{9} =$ **3.** $\frac{1}{6} + \frac{1}{6} =$

4. $\frac{3}{6} + \frac{1}{6} =$ **5.** $\frac{2}{4} + \frac{2}{4} =$ **6.** $\frac{1}{2} + \frac{1}{2} =$

7. $\frac{5}{8} + \frac{3}{8} =$ **8.** $\frac{5}{5} + \frac{2}{5} =$ **9.** $\frac{2}{10} + \frac{4}{10} =$

10. $\frac{1}{4} + \frac{3}{4} =$ **11.** $\frac{3}{5} + \frac{2}{5} =$ **12.** $\frac{3}{7} + \frac{2}{7} =$

13. $\frac{3}{4} + \frac{1}{4} =$ **14.** $\frac{1}{7} + \frac{1}{7} =$ **15.** $\frac{1}{6} + \frac{4}{6} =$

                                   CD-104320 • © Carson-Dellosa

Addition of Fractions

Solve each problem. Write the answer in its simplest form.

Have Fun with Fractions!

1. $\dfrac{2}{7}$
    $+\dfrac{3}{7}$

2. $\dfrac{6}{8}$
    $+\dfrac{1}{8}$

3. $\dfrac{7}{10}$
    $+\dfrac{9}{10}$

4. $\dfrac{3}{7}$
    $+\dfrac{1}{7}$

5. $\dfrac{1}{5}$
    $+\dfrac{3}{5}$

6. $\dfrac{3}{5}$
    $+\dfrac{3}{5}$

7. $\dfrac{1}{4}$
    $+\dfrac{2}{4}$

8. $\dfrac{1}{5}$
    $+\dfrac{3}{5}$

9. $\dfrac{4}{8}$
    $+\dfrac{2}{8}$

10. $\dfrac{6}{7}$
    $+\dfrac{5}{7}$

11. $\dfrac{1}{8}$
    $+\dfrac{5}{8}$

12. $\dfrac{2}{8}$
    $+\dfrac{4}{8}$

13. $\dfrac{2}{10}$
    $+\dfrac{4}{10}$

14. $\dfrac{3}{4}$
    $+\dfrac{2}{4}$

15. $\dfrac{2}{3}$
    $+\dfrac{1}{3}$

16. $\dfrac{4}{9}$
    $+\dfrac{3}{9}$

17. $\dfrac{2}{6}$
    $+\dfrac{1}{6}$

18. $\dfrac{5}{12}$
    $+\dfrac{5}{12}$

19. $\dfrac{1}{6}$
    $+\dfrac{3}{6}$

20. $\dfrac{2}{9}$
    $+\dfrac{1}{9}$

Subtraction with Numbers Through 12

Total Problems: **33**
Problems Correct: _____

Solve each problem.

Take Subtraction for a Spin!

1. 4
   − 0

2. 12
   − 4

3. 4
   − 2

4. 7
   − 3

5. 2
   − 1

6. 11
   − 4

7. 9
   − 2

8. 7
   − 4

9. 3
   − 3

10. 11
   − 3

11. 5
   − 3

12. 6
   − 2

13. 6
   − 3

14. 10
   − 2

15. 3
   − 2

16. 11
   − 3

17. 5
   − 2

18. 4
   − 1

19. 12
   − 3

20. 7
   − 2

21. 6
   − 4

22. 8
   − 4

23. 2
   − 0

24. 10
   − 3

25. 8
   − 2

26. 3
   − 1

27. 8
   − 1

28. 10
   − 3

29. 9
   − 3

30. 9
   − 4

31. 8
   − 4

32. 4
   − 3

33. 10
   − 7

Name _____ Date _____

Subtraction with Numbers Through 18

Total Problems: **33**
Problems Correct: _____

Solve each problem.

You Can Handle It!

1. 15
 − 8

2. 11
 − 6

3. 14
 − 7

4. 10
 − 6

5. 8
 − 0

6. 12
 − 7

7. 12
 − 5

8. 14
 − 8

9. 10
 − 7

10. 8
 − 6

11. 13
 − 8

12. 9
 − 6

13. 6
 − 0

14. 16
 − 7

15. 7
 − 0

16. 7
 − 5

17. 15
 − 6

18. 10
 − 8

19. 16
 − 6

20. 8
 − 1

21. 12
 − 8

22. 18
 − 8

23. 8
 − 8

24. 9
 − 7

25. 7
 − 1

26. 13
 − 6

27. 6
 − 1

28. 14
 − 6

29. 14
 − 7

30. 7
 − 6

31. 9
 − 8

32. 10
 − 7

33. 8
 − 3

Subtraction with Numbers Through 19

Total Problems: **33**
Problems Correct: _____

Solve each problem.

Take Your Time!

1. 18
  − 9

2. 12
  − 8

3. 15
  − 8

4. 13
  − 9

5. 17
  − 9

6. 17
  − 8

7. 16
  − 9

8. 9
  − 9

9. 7
  − 7

10. 13
  − 7

11. 19
  − 8

12. 14
  − 7

13. 11
  − 7

14. 8
  − 7

15. 14
  − 8

16. 13
  − 8

17. 11
  − 9

18. 15
  − 7

19. 16
  − 8

20. 10
  − 8

21. 9
  − 1

22. 12
  − 9

23. 10
  − 7

24. 16
  − 8

25. 11
  − 8

26. 12
  − 9

27. 12
  − 7

28. 9
  − 7

29. 17
  − 7

30. 17
  − 9

31. 14
  − 9

32. 16
  − 9

33. 14
  − 9

     CD-104320 • © Carson-Dellosa

Subtraction with Numbers Through 19

Solve each problem.

Time to Subtract!

1. 4 − 3	**2.** 7 − 3	**3.** 13 − 6	**4.** 5 − 3	**5.** 19 − 4	**6.** 15 − 7
7. 17 − 8	**8.** 9 − 2	**9.** 15 − 8	**10.** 11 − 6	**11.** 16 − 9	**12.** 8 − 1
13. 8 − 5	**14.** 9 − 4	**15.** 6 − 2	**16.** 18 − 7	**17.** 7 − 2	**18.** 12 − 8
19. 12 − 7	**20.** 9 − 6	**21.** 9 − 1	**22.** 10 − 5	**23.** 14 − 9	**24.** 8 − 4
25. 13 − 9	**26.** 6 − 4	**27.** 11 − 5	**28.** 14 − 8	**29.** 15 − 6	**30.** 19 − 9
31. 16 − 7	**32.** 14 − 5	**33.** 6 − 1			

Two-Digit Subtraction

Solve each problem.

Give Subtraction a Whirl!

1. 82 – 31	**2.** 88 – 32	**3.** 86 – 51	**4.** 67 – 42	**5.** 75 – 25	**6.** 94 – 60
7. 98 – 77	**8.** 64 – 31	**9.** 37 – 22	**10.** 48 – 24	**11.** 56 – 22	**12.** 28 – 15
13. 75 – 42	**14.** 88 – 66	**15.** 87 – 33	**16.** 99 – 65	**17.** 78 – 41	**18.** 61 – 30
19. 65 – 32	**20.** 93 – 52	**21.** 88 – 35	**22.** 85 – 73	**23.** 95 – 62	**24.** 74 – 42
25. 36 – 15	**26.** 75 – 53	**27.** 76 – 51	**28.** 73 – 21	**29.** 39 – 12	**30.** 58 – 33
31. 43 – 31	**32.** 67 – 12	**33.** 85 – 31			

Name _____   Date _____

Two-Digit Subtraction with Regrouping

Solve each problem. Regroup when necessary.

Subtraction Is a Breeze!

1. 86
   − 38

2. 73
   − 45

3. 53
   − 37

4. 48
   − 29

5. 76
   − 68

6. 64
   − 48

7. 94
   − 58

8. 42
   − 27

9. 81
   − 53

10. 66
    − 38

11. 78
    − 59

12. 72
    − 47

13. 66
    − 38

14. 97
    − 58

15. 67
    − 18

16. 66
    − 49

17. 57
    − 29

18. 36
    − 19

19. 55
    − 49

20. 55
    − 26

21. 78
    − 49

22. 91
    − 73

23. 90
    − 33

24. 86
    − 27

25. 31
    − 23

26. 46
    − 29

27. 66
    − 47

28. 74
    − 35

29. 28
    − 19

30. 63
    − 45

31. 76
    − 49

32. 70
    − 27

33. 56
    − 39

Two- and Three-Digit Subtraction with Regrouping

Total Problems: **33**
Problems Correct: _____

Solve each problem. Regroup when necessary.

Moo-ving Right Along!

1. 95
  − 66

2. 812
  − 726

3. 434
  − 356

4. 769
  − 438

5. 879
  − 389

6. 49
  − 24

7. 53
  − 27

8. 82
  − 38

9. 87
  − 78

10. 726
  − 417

11. 75
  − 58

12. 87
  − 39

13. 93
  − 46

14. 78
  − 39

15. 612
  − 538

16. 800
  − 524

17. 539
  − 366

18. 576
  − 379

19. 658
  − 377

20. 632
  − 167

21. 936
  − 687

22. 841
  − 385

23. 695
  − 289

24. 625
  − 378

25. 768
  − 579

26. 798
  − 599

27. 473
  − 128

28. 635
  − 574

29. 484
  − 299

30. 832
  − 597

31. 837
  − 376

32. 536
  − 359

33. 938
  − 377

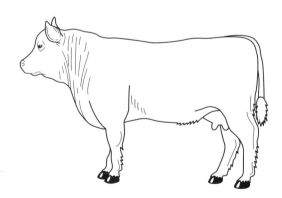

Three-Digit Subtraction with Regrouping

Solve each problem. Regroup when necessary.

Don't Have a Cow!

1. 736 − 397	**2.** 890 − 249	**3.** 768 − 479	**4.** 385 − 269	**5.** 747 − 458	**6.** 837 − 209
7. 476 − 267	**8.** 689 − 478	**9.** 677 − 288	**10.** 376 − 187	**11.** 521 − 294	**12.** 387 − 329
13. 301 − 242	**14.** 541 − 377	**15.** 471 − 382	**16.** 727 − 419	**17.** 848 − 399	**18.** 847 − 358
19. 502 − 321	**20.** 704 − 597	**21.** 846 − 457	**22.** 603 − 277	**23.** 405 − 228	**24.** 235 − 128
25. 703 − 478	**26.** 787 − 548	**27.** 584 − 295	**28.** 600 − 367	**29.** 400 − 373	**30.** 548 − 369
31. 834 − 657	**32.** 748 − 259	**33.** 748 − 459			

Name _____   Date _____

Three-Digit Subtraction with Regrouping

Solve each problem. Regroup when necessary.

Relax with Subtraction!

1. 784
   − 591

2. 547
   − 265

3. 622
   − 323

4. 825
   − 638

5. 923
   − 568

6. 950
   − 580

7. 663
   − 271

8. 967
   − 794

9. 982
   − 398

10. 293
    − 187

11. 732
    − 467

12. 824
    − 548

13. 845
    − 566

14. 429
    − 188

15. 659
    − 478

16. 725
    − 469

17. 827
    − 577

18. 536
    − 459

19. 527
    − 265

20. 574
    − 293

21. 557
    − 278

22. 423
    − 155

23. 766
    − 577

24. 536
    − 258

25. 677
    − 289

26. 857
    − 675

27. 783
    − 399

28. 748
    − 353

29. 831
    − 357

30. 521
    − 245

31. 940
    − 565

32. 438
    − 254

33. 487
    − 378

Three- and Four-Digit Subtraction with Regrouping

Solve each problem. Regroup when necessary.

Take It Easy!

1. 653
    − 277

2. 8,564
    − 3,956

3. 4,856
    − 2,789

4. 3,111
    − 1,278

5. 527
    − 386

6. 3,956
    − 2,597

7. 7,775
    − 4,959

8. 3,834
    − 3,675

9. 845
    − 608

10. 8,945
     − 4,867

11. 4,831
     − 1,945

12. 8,352
     − 2,777

13. 263
     − 157

14. 751
     − 397

15. 9,276
     − 5,983

16. 5,650
     − 4,584

17. 6,120
     − 3,212

18. 414
     − 347

19. 629
     − 563

20. 9,634
     − 7,985

21. 3,481
     − 2,349

22. 8,543
     − 4,199

23. 437
     − 167

24. 438
     − 289

25. 4,483
     − 2,659

26. 7,433
     − 1,389

27. 4,392
     − 2,899

Four-Digit Subtraction with Regrouping

Solve each problem. Regroup when necessary.

Shoot for the Moon!

1. 9,534 – 2,389	**2.** 5,464 – 2,756	**3.** 3,526 – 1,653	**4.** 3,354 – 2,328	**5.** 5,247 –3,836	**6.** 8,456 – 3,462
7. 4,755 – 3,875	**8.** 7,243 – 2,376	**9.** 6,845 – 4,764	**10.** 5,935 – 3,837	**11.** 4,376 – 2,438	**12.** 9,122 – 4,547
13. 2,643 – 1,439	**14.** 3,765 – 3,498	**15.** 7,236 – 2,276	**16.** 7,340 – 5,364	**17.** 6,849 – 4,114	**18.** 7,414 – 2,838
19. 6,249 – 5,633	**20.** 8,344 – 4,754	**21.** 8,363 – 6,476	**22.** 7,221 – 5,347	**23.** 4,343 – 3,278	**24.** 3,567 – 2,853
25. 5,277 – 1,654	**26.** 9,644 – 5,842	**27.** 6,694 – 4,851			

Four-Digit Subtraction

Total Problems: **27**
Problems Correct: _____

Solve each problem. Regroup when necessary.

You're a Star!

1. 7,687 – 2,438	**2.** 3,465 – 1,854	**3.** 6,895 – 2,957	**4.** 4,568 – 3,489	**5.** 7,264 – 6,966	**6.** 8,346 – 6,478
7. 6,894 – 2,785	**8.** 7,945 – 3,329	**9.** 2,348 – 1,365	**10.** 8,232 – 3,984	**11.** 6,189 – 2,312	**12.** 8,909 – 7,498
13. 4,879 – 2,782	**14.** 7,493 – 4,691	**15.** 6,349 – 2,542	**16.** 4,393 – 2,765	**17.** 9,347 – 3,659	**18.** 8,785 – 4,934
19. 7,946 – 7,745	**20.** 8,238 – 7,459	**21.** 4,319 – 2,880	**22.** 3,769 – 2,424	**23.** 4,111 – 2,648	**24.** 4,846 – 2,845
25. 8,945 – 5,289	**26.** 4,349 – 2,375	**27.** 3,020 – 2,303			

Name _____   Date _____

Five-Digit Subtraction

Total Problems: **27**
Problems Correct: _____

Solve each problem. Regroup when necessary.

Hang in There!

1. 34,347 – 23,564	2. 54,347 – 35,756	3. 53,768 – 44,768	4. 68,498 – 56,856	5. 59,547 – 48,945	6. 78,345 – 43,274

7. 86,423 – 83,575	8. 65,567 – 56,980	9. 72,894 – 67,989	10. 78,960 – 56,809	11. 76,378 – 35,789	12. 43,698 – 25,435

13. 76,453 – 47,456	14. 78,498 – 56,843	15. 56,896 – 52,908	16. 43,645 – 34,883	17. 64,348 – 21,212	18. 98,456 – 89,564

19. 76,196 – 56,456	20. 88,067 – 34,980	21. 23,999 – 21,938	22. 74,665 – 43,883	23. 76,486 – 56,758	24. 35,348 – 12,340

25. 32,675 – 27,456	26. 87,906 – 56,945	27. 63,921 – 56,712

Name _____   Date _____

Subtraction of Decimals

Solve each problem. Regroup when necessary.

Don't Bat an Eye at Subtraction!

1. 7.36
    − 3.97

2. 8.90
    − 2.49

3. 7.68
    − 4.79

4. 3.85
    − 2.79

5. 7.47
    − 4.58

6. 8.37
    − 2.09

7. 4.76
    − 2.67

8. 6.89
    − 4.78

9. 6.77
    − 2.88

10. 3.76
    − 1.87

11. 5.21
    − 2.94

12. 3.87
    − 3.29

13. 3.01
    − 2.42

14. 5.41
    − 3.77

15. 4.71
    − 3.82

16. 7.27
    − 4.19

17. 8.48
    − 3.99

18. 8.47
    − 3.58

19. 5.02
    − 3.21

20. 7.04
    − 6.67

21. 8.46
    − 4.57

22. 6.03
    − 2.77

23. 4.05
    − 2.28

24. 2.35
    − 1.28

25. 7.03
    − 4.78

26. 7.87
    − 5.48

27. 5.84
    − 2.95

28. 6.00
    − 3.67

29. 4.00
    − 3.73

30. 5.48
    − 3.69

31. 8.34
    − 6.57

32. 7.48
    − 2.59

33. 7.48
    − 4.59

Subtraction of Decimals

Solve each problem. Regroup when necessary.

You're Doing Swimmingly!

1. 7.84
− 5.91

2. 5.47
− 2.65

3. 6.22
− 3.23

4. 8.25
− 6.38

5. 9.23
− 5.68

6. 9.50
− 5.80

7. 6.63
− 2.61

8. 9.67
− 7.94

9. 9.82
− 3.98

10. 2.93
− 1.87

11. 7.32
− 4.67

12. 8.24
− 5.48

13. 8.45
− 5.66

14. 4.29
− 1.88

15. 6.59
− 4.78

16. 7.25
− 4.69

17. 8.27
− 6.45

18. 5.36
− 4.59

19. 5.27
− 2.65

20. 5.74
− 2.93

21. 5.57
− 2.78

22. 4.23
− 1.55

23. 7.66
− 5.77

24. 5.36
− 2.58

25. 6.77
− 2.89

26. 8.57
− 6.75

27. 7.86
− 3.89

28. 7.48
− 3.53

29. 8.31
− 3.57

30. 5.12
− 2.45

31. 9.40
− 5.65

32. 4.38
− 2.54

33. 4.87
− 3.78

Subtraction of Fractions

Solve each problem. Write each answer in its simplest form.

Fishing for Answers!

1. $\dfrac{5}{6}$
    $-\dfrac{4}{6}$

2. $\dfrac{4}{7}$
    $-\dfrac{2}{7}$

3. $\dfrac{3}{5}$
    $-\dfrac{2}{5}$

4. $\dfrac{10}{11}$
    $-\dfrac{5}{11}$

5. $\dfrac{5}{8}$
    $-\dfrac{1}{8}$

6. $\dfrac{4}{5}$
    $-\dfrac{3}{5}$

7. $\dfrac{3}{6}$
    $-\dfrac{2}{6}$

8. $\dfrac{3}{4}$
    $-\dfrac{2}{4}$

9. $\dfrac{7}{10}$
    $-\dfrac{2}{10}$

10. $\dfrac{7}{8}$
    $-\dfrac{4}{8}$

11. $\dfrac{1}{3}$
    $-\dfrac{1}{3}$

12. $\dfrac{7}{8}$
    $-\dfrac{2}{8}$

13. $\dfrac{4}{9}$
    $-\dfrac{2}{9}$

14. $\dfrac{9}{11}$
    $-\dfrac{1}{11}$

15. $\dfrac{4}{10}$
    $-\dfrac{3}{10}$

16. $\dfrac{8}{12}$
    $-\dfrac{5}{12}$

17. $\dfrac{3}{8}$
    $-\dfrac{1}{8}$

18. $\dfrac{4}{7}$
    $-\dfrac{1}{7}$

19. $\dfrac{8}{9}$
    $-\dfrac{2}{9}$

20. $\dfrac{4}{5}$
    $-\dfrac{1}{5}$

21. $\dfrac{9}{12}$
    $-\dfrac{2}{12}$

22. $\dfrac{8}{11}$
    $-\dfrac{2}{11}$

23. $\dfrac{6}{7}$
    $-\dfrac{1}{7}$

24. $\dfrac{8}{10}$
    $-\dfrac{2}{10}$

Name _____   Date _____

Multiplication with the Factor 2

Solve each problem.

Total Problems: **33**
Problems Correct: _____

Catch on to Multiplication!

1. 2
  × 3

2. 2
  × 7

3. 2
  × 1

4. 2
  × 2

5. 3
  × 2

6. 9
  × 2

7. 7
  × 2

8. 3
  × 2

9. 6
  × 2

10. 1
  × 2

11. 4
  × 2

12. 2
  × 0

13. 0
  × 2

14. 2
  × 4

15. 2
  × 6

16. 2
  × 2

17. 2
  × 3

18. 5
  × 2

19. 2
  × 4

20. 2
  × 7

21. 5
  × 2

22. 2
  × 8

23. 7
  × 2

24. 2
  × 8

25. 2
  × 5

26. 2
  × 2

27. 2
  × 9

28. 6
  × 2

29. 2
  × 5

30. 7
  × 2

31. 2
  × 1

32. 7
  × 2

33. 2
  × 3

36

CD-104320 • © Carson-Dellosa

Name _____ Date _____

Multiplication with Factors 0–2

Solve each problem.

You've Got It!

1. 9
    × 1

2. 1
    × 2

3. 7
    × 0

4. 3
    × 2

5. 2
    × 0

6. 2
    × 8

7. 6
    × 2

8. 1
    × 8

9. 5
    × 2

10. 9
     × 2

11. 4
     × 2

12. 5
     × 1

13. 2
     × 1

14. 6
     × 0

15. 6
     × 1

16. 2
     × 8

17. 8
     × 0

18. 7
     × 2

19. 3
     × 0

20. 4
     × 2

21. 1
     × 0

22. 4
     × 0

23. 2
     × 2

24. 4
     × 1

25. 5
     × 0

26. 1
     × 7

27. 3
     × 2

28. 2
     × 9

29. 0
     × 1

30. 2
     × 6

31. 1
     × 9

32. 0
     × 2

33. 1
     × 1

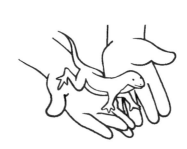

Name _____   Date _____

Multiplication with the Factor 3

Solve each problem.

Roll Through Multiplication!

1. 3
   ×7

2. 3
   ×8

3. 9
   ×3

4. 4
   ×3

5. 3
   ×9

6. 3
   ×5

7. 4
   ×3

8. 3
   ×7

9. 1
   ×3

10. 3
    ×3

11. 6
    ×3

12. 7
    ×3

13. 3
    ×9

14. 8
    ×3

15. 3
    ×6

16. 3
    ×3

17. 3
    ×5

18. 5
    ×3

19. 2
    ×3

20. 3
    ×3

21. 3
    ×4

22. 9
    ×3

23. 3
    ×0

24. 3
    ×1

25. 2
    ×3

26. 3
    ×2

27. 8
    ×3

28. 3
    ×4

29. 3
    ×6

30. 6
    ×3

31. 3
    ×8

32. 7
    ×3

33. 0
    ×3

Name _____ Date _____

Multiplication with Factors 2 and 3

Total Problems: **33**
Problems Correct: _____

Solve each problem.

You're on a Roll!

1. 3 ×9	**2.** 3 ×0	**3.** 2 ×1	**4.** 3 ×2	**5.** 8 ×3	**6.** 3 ×7

1. 3
×9

2. 3
×0

3. 2
×1

4. 3
×2

5. 8
×3

6. 3
×7

7. 3
×4

8. 3
×8

9. 4
×3

10. 2
×2

11. 2
×3

12. 2
×6

13. 2
×0

14. 1
×2

15. 0
×3

16. 3
×5

17. 5
×2

18. 2
×7

19. 3
×3

20. 9
×3

21. 3
×6

22. 4
×2

23. 5
×3

24. 7
×3

25. 6
×2

26. 6
×3

27. 3
×3

28. 7
×2

29. 2
×8

30. 2
×9

31. 9
×2

32. 8
×2

33. 2
×4

Multiplication with the Factor 4

Solve each problem.

You're on Your Way Up!

1. $\begin{array}{r} 9 \\ \times 4 \\ \hline \end{array}$
2. $\begin{array}{r} 4 \\ \times 8 \\ \hline \end{array}$
3. $\begin{array}{r} 7 \\ \times 4 \\ \hline \end{array}$
4. $\begin{array}{r} 4 \\ \times 7 \\ \hline \end{array}$
5. $\begin{array}{r} 6 \\ \times 4 \\ \hline \end{array}$
6. $\begin{array}{r} 4 \\ \times 5 \\ \hline \end{array}$

7. $\begin{array}{r} 4 \\ \times 2 \\ \hline \end{array}$
8. $\begin{array}{r} 3 \\ \times 4 \\ \hline \end{array}$
9. $\begin{array}{r} 4 \\ \times 3 \\ \hline \end{array}$
10. $\begin{array}{r} 4 \\ \times 1 \\ \hline \end{array}$
11. $\begin{array}{r} 8 \\ \times 4 \\ \hline \end{array}$
12. $\begin{array}{r} 4 \\ \times 9 \\ \hline \end{array}$

13. $\begin{array}{r} 4 \\ \times 6 \\ \hline \end{array}$
14. $\begin{array}{r} 1 \\ \times 4 \\ \hline \end{array}$
15. $\begin{array}{r} 4 \\ \times 2 \\ \hline \end{array}$
16. $\begin{array}{r} 2 \\ \times 4 \\ \hline \end{array}$
17. $\begin{array}{r} 4 \\ \times 4 \\ \hline \end{array}$
18. $\begin{array}{r} 7 \\ \times 4 \\ \hline \end{array}$

19. $\begin{array}{r} 4 \\ \times 0 \\ \hline \end{array}$
20. $\begin{array}{r} 4 \\ \times 9 \\ \hline \end{array}$
21. $\begin{array}{r} 7 \\ \times 4 \\ \hline \end{array}$
22. $\begin{array}{r} 4 \\ \times 6 \\ \hline \end{array}$
23. $\begin{array}{r} 4 \\ \times 5 \\ \hline \end{array}$
24. $\begin{array}{r} 4 \\ \times 9 \\ \hline \end{array}$

25. $\begin{array}{r} 4 \\ \times 4 \\ \hline \end{array}$
26. $\begin{array}{r} 4 \\ \times 8 \\ \hline \end{array}$
27. $\begin{array}{r} 0 \\ \times 4 \\ \hline \end{array}$
28. $\begin{array}{r} 4 \\ \times 5 \\ \hline \end{array}$
29. $\begin{array}{r} 4 \\ \times 7 \\ \hline \end{array}$
30. $\begin{array}{r} 5 \\ \times 4 \\ \hline \end{array}$

31. $\begin{array}{r} 8 \\ \times 4 \\ \hline \end{array}$
32. $\begin{array}{r} 9 \\ \times 4 \\ \hline \end{array}$
33. $\begin{array}{r} 4 \\ \times 9 \\ \hline \end{array}$

Multiplication with Factors 2–4

Solve each problem.

Get a Leg Up on Math!

1. 7
   ×4

2. 8
   ×4

3. 4
   ×9

4. 5
   ×4

5. 2
   ×3

6. 4
   ×2

7. 3
   ×2

8. 3
   ×1

9. 6
   ×2

10. 3
    ×5

11. 8
    ×3

12. 8
    ×4

13. 3
    ×3

14. 4
    ×4

15. 5
    ×2

16. 6
    ×4

17. 12
    ×2

18. 7
    ×3

19. 3
    ×6

20. 8
    ×3

21. 3
    ×3

22. 2
    ×9

23. 1
    ×4

24. 3
    ×2

25. 2
    ×2

26. 2
    ×4

27. 9
    ×4

28. 1
    ×3

29. 2
    ×8

30. 3
    ×5

31. 1
    ×4

32. 2
    ×7

33. 4
    ×5

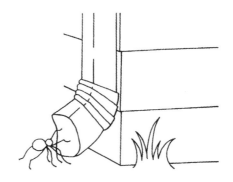

Multiplication with the Factor 5

Solve each problem.

The Sweet Rewards of Math!

1. $\begin{array}{r} 5 \\ \times\,7 \\ \hline \end{array}$
2. $\begin{array}{r} 5 \\ \times\,9 \\ \hline \end{array}$
3. $\begin{array}{r} 6 \\ \times\,5 \\ \hline \end{array}$
4. $\begin{array}{r} 0 \\ \times\,5 \\ \hline \end{array}$
5. $\begin{array}{r} 5 \\ \times\,8 \\ \hline \end{array}$
6. $\begin{array}{r} 5 \\ \times\,0 \\ \hline \end{array}$

7. $\begin{array}{r} 2 \\ \times\,5 \\ \hline \end{array}$
8. $\begin{array}{r} 7 \\ \times\,5 \\ \hline \end{array}$
9. $\begin{array}{r} 9 \\ \times\,5 \\ \hline \end{array}$
10. $\begin{array}{r} 5 \\ \times\,3 \\ \hline \end{array}$
11. $\begin{array}{r} 5 \\ \times\,6 \\ \hline \end{array}$
12. $\begin{array}{r} 5 \\ \times\,7 \\ \hline \end{array}$

13. $\begin{array}{r} 2 \\ \times\,5 \\ \hline \end{array}$
14. $\begin{array}{r} 5 \\ \times\,5 \\ \hline \end{array}$
15. $\begin{array}{r} 5 \\ \times\,4 \\ \hline \end{array}$
16. $\begin{array}{r} 4 \\ \times\,5 \\ \hline \end{array}$
17. $\begin{array}{r} 5 \\ \times\,2 \\ \hline \end{array}$
18. $\begin{array}{r} 9 \\ \times\,5 \\ \hline \end{array}$

19. $\begin{array}{r} 4 \\ \times\,5 \\ \hline \end{array}$
20. $\begin{array}{r} 8 \\ \times\,5 \\ \hline \end{array}$
21. $\begin{array}{r} 1 \\ \times\,5 \\ \hline \end{array}$
22. $\begin{array}{r} 5 \\ \times\,5 \\ \hline \end{array}$
23. $\begin{array}{r} 3 \\ \times\,5 \\ \hline \end{array}$
24. $\begin{array}{r} 5 \\ \times\,6 \\ \hline \end{array}$

25. $\begin{array}{r} 5 \\ \times\,8 \\ \hline \end{array}$
26. $\begin{array}{r} 5 \\ \times\,4 \\ \hline \end{array}$
27. $\begin{array}{r} 6 \\ \times\,5 \\ \hline \end{array}$
28. $\begin{array}{r} 5 \\ \times\,5 \\ \hline \end{array}$
29. $\begin{array}{r} 5 \\ \times\,3 \\ \hline \end{array}$
30. $\begin{array}{r} 5 \\ \times\,1 \\ \hline \end{array}$

31. $\begin{array}{r} 5 \\ \times\,2 \\ \hline \end{array}$
32. $\begin{array}{r} 5 \\ \times\,9 \\ \hline \end{array}$
33. $\begin{array}{r} 9 \\ \times\,5 \\ \hline \end{array}$

Multiplication with Factors 4 and 5

Solve each problem.

Be a Busy Bee!

1. 5
   $\times$ 6

2. 5
   $\times$ 7

3. 5
   $\times$ 8

4. 8
   $\times$ 5

5. 2
   $\times$ 5

6. 3
   $\times$ 5

7. 4
   $\times$ 8

8. 4
   $\times$ 2

9. 5
   $\times$ 5

10. 8
   $\times$ 4

11. 4
   $\times$ 9

12. 4
   $\times$ 1

13. 5
   $\times$ 3

14. 0
   $\times$ 4

15. 7
   $\times$ 5

16. 9
   $\times$ 5

17. 3
   $\times$ 4

18. 5
   $\times$ 5

19. 7
   $\times$ 4

20. 5
   $\times$ 2

21. 1
   $\times$ 5

22. 4
   $\times$ 7

23. 5
   $\times$ 9

24. 5
   $\times$ 3

25. 6
   $\times$ 4

26. 4
   $\times$ 2

27. 1
   $\times$ 4

28. 4
   $\times$ 3

29. 6
   $\times$ 5

30. 5
   $\times$ 4

31. 9
   $\times$ 4

32. 4
   $\times$ 5

33. 4
   $\times$ 6

Multiplication with Factors 2–5

Solve each problem.

Total Problems:	**33**
Problems Correct:	_____

Swinging Through Multiplication!

1. 2
$\times 5$

2. 5
$\times 8$

3. 5
$\times 3$

4. 8
$\times 4$

5. 3
$\times 4$

6. 7
$\times 2$

7. 7
$\times 5$

8. 1
$\times 4$

9. 3
$\times 5$

10. 2
$\times 2$

11. 8
$\times 3$

12. 4
$\times 3$

13. 4
$\times 6$

14. 5
$\times 2$

15. 4
$\times 5$

16. 2
$\times 9$

17. 5
$\times 5$

18. 5
$\times 6$

19. 4
$\times 2$

20. 4
$\times 9$

21. 9
$\times 3$

22. 4
$\times 4$

23. 3
$\times 7$

24. 8
$\times 2$

25. 6
$\times 2$

26. 3
$\times 6$

27. 2
$\times 4$

28. 4
$\times 7$

29. 3
$\times 2$

30. 9
$\times 5$

31. 5
$\times 1$

32. 2
$\times 3$

33. 3
$\times 1$

Multiplication with the Factor 6

Solve each problem.

Hanging Around with Math!

1. 8
   × 6

2. 2
   × 6

3. 7
   × 6

4. 6
   × 5

5. 5
   × 6

6. 6
   × 7

7. 8
   × 6

8. 6
   × 3

9. 6
   × 8

10. 6
   × 4

11. 5
   × 6

12. 6
   × 0

13. 8
   × 6

14. 4
   × 6

15. 2
   × 6

16. 6
   × 6

17. 3
   × 6

18. 6
   × 3

19. 6
   × 4

20. 6
   × 9

21. 7
   × 6

22. 6
   × 1

23. 6
   × 2

24. 6
   × 9

25. 6
   × 6

26. 6
   × 3

27. 6
   × 5

28. 9
   × 6

29. 6
   × 8

30. 1
   × 6

31. 3
   × 6

32. 6
   × 6

33. 9
   × 6

Multiplication with the Factor 7

Solve each problem.

Soar Through Multiplication!

1. $\begin{array}{r} 0 \\ \times 7 \\ \hline \end{array}$ 2. $\begin{array}{r} 8 \\ \times 7 \\ \hline \end{array}$ 3. $\begin{array}{r} 2 \\ \times 7 \\ \hline \end{array}$ 4. $\begin{array}{r} 7 \\ \times 7 \\ \hline \end{array}$ 5. $\begin{array}{r} 7 \\ \times 5 \\ \hline \end{array}$ 6. $\begin{array}{r} 7 \\ \times 8 \\ \hline \end{array}$

7. $\begin{array}{r} 7 \\ \times 7 \\ \hline \end{array}$ 8. $\begin{array}{r} 7 \\ \times 2 \\ \hline \end{array}$ 9. $\begin{array}{r} 9 \\ \times 7 \\ \hline \end{array}$ 10. $\begin{array}{r} 7 \\ \times 9 \\ \hline \end{array}$ 11. $\begin{array}{r} 4 \\ \times 7 \\ \hline \end{array}$ 12. $\begin{array}{r} 1 \\ \times 7 \\ \hline \end{array}$

13. $\begin{array}{r} 8 \\ \times 7 \\ \hline \end{array}$ 14. $\begin{array}{r} 3 \\ \times 7 \\ \hline \end{array}$ 15. $\begin{array}{r} 6 \\ \times 7 \\ \hline \end{array}$ 16. $\begin{array}{r} 7 \\ \times 4 \\ \hline \end{array}$ 17. $\begin{array}{r} 5 \\ \times 7 \\ \hline \end{array}$ 18. $\begin{array}{r} 4 \\ \times 7 \\ \hline \end{array}$

19. $\begin{array}{r} 5 \\ \times 7 \\ \hline \end{array}$ 20. $\begin{array}{r} 7 \\ \times 4 \\ \hline \end{array}$ 21. $\begin{array}{r} 7 \\ \times 0 \\ \hline \end{array}$ 22. $\begin{array}{r} 7 \\ \times 2 \\ \hline \end{array}$ 23. $\begin{array}{r} 7 \\ \times 8 \\ \hline \end{array}$ 24. $\begin{array}{r} 7 \\ \times 9 \\ \hline \end{array}$

25. $\begin{array}{r} 2 \\ \times 7 \\ \hline \end{array}$ 26. $\begin{array}{r} 7 \\ \times 6 \\ \hline \end{array}$ 27. $\begin{array}{r} 7 \\ \times 2 \\ \hline \end{array}$ 28. $\begin{array}{r} 6 \\ \times 7 \\ \hline \end{array}$ 29. $\begin{array}{r} 7 \\ \times 3 \\ \hline \end{array}$ 30. $\begin{array}{r} 7 \\ \times 5 \\ \hline \end{array}$

31. $\begin{array}{r} 7 \\ \times 6 \\ \hline \end{array}$ 32. $\begin{array}{r} 7 \\ \times 7 \\ \hline \end{array}$ 33. $\begin{array}{r} 7 \\ \times 3 \\ \hline \end{array}$

   CD-104320 • © Carson-Dellosa

Multiplication with Factors 6 and 7

Total Problems: **33**
Problems Correct: _____

Solve each problem.

Spread Your Wings!

1. 3
×7

2. 7
×8

3. 9
×7

4. 9
×6

5. 1
×7

6. 6
×8

7. 6
×4

8. 8
×6

9. 8
×7

10. 2
×6

11. 7
×5

12. 4
×6

13. 0
×7

14. 7
×4

15. 6
×6

16. 1
×6

17. 3
×6

18. 7
×2

19. 7
×7

20. 5
×6

21. 2
×7

22. 6
×9

23. 4
×7

24. 7
×9

25. 3
×6

26. 6
×7

27. 6
×5

28. 7
×7

29. 6
×6

30. 6
×3

31. 7
×6

32. 0
×6

33. 5
×7

Multiplication with the Factor 8

Solve each problem.

Total Problems: **33**
Problems Correct: _____

Way to Go!

1. 8
  × 9

2. 7
  × 8

3. 4
  × 8

4. 0
  × 8

5. 8
  × 6

6. 8
  × 0

7. 8
  × 8

8. 1
  × 8

9. 9
  × 8

10. 2
   × 8

11. 8
   × 3

12. 8
   × 4

13. 6
   × 8

14. 8
   × 5

15. 5
   × 8

16. 2
   × 8

17. 9
   × 8

18. 8
   × 8

19. 4
   × 8

20. 8
   × 3

21. 8
   × 2

22. 2
   × 8

23. 8
   × 5

24. 3
   × 8

25. 8
   × 2

26. 8
   × 9

27. 9
   × 8

28. 8
   × 7

29. 8
   × 1

30. 8
   × 6

31. 8
   × 7

32. 8
   × 4

33. 8
   × 5

CD-104320 • © Carson-Dellosa

Multiplication with the Factor 9

Solve each problem.

Nice Job!

1. 5
   ×9

2. 9
   ×3

3. 9
   ×9

4. 9
   ×1

5. 0
   ×9

6. 9
   ×9

7. 9
   ×8

8. 5
   ×9

9. 9
   ×2

10. 9
    ×8

11. 3
    ×9

12. 9
    ×6

13. 9
    ×9

14. 9
    ×4

15. 5
    ×9

16. 6
    ×9

17. 9
    ×2

18. 2
    ×9

19. 9
    ×5

20. 9
    ×9

21. 3
    ×9

22. 8
    ×9

23. 9
    ×7

24. 9
    ×0

25. 9
    ×3

26. 9
    ×7

27. 1
    ×9

28. 9
    ×4

29. 2
    ×9

30. 4
    ×9

31. 8
    ×9

32. 4
    ×9

33. 6
    ×9

Multiplication with Factors 8 and 9

Solve each problem.

Put Your Mind to It!

1. $\begin{array}{r} 9 \\ \times 7 \\ \hline \end{array}$ 2. $\begin{array}{r} 4 \\ \times 8 \\ \hline \end{array}$ 3. $\begin{array}{r} 9 \\ \times 5 \\ \hline \end{array}$ 4. $\begin{array}{r} 6 \\ \times 8 \\ \hline \end{array}$ 5. $\begin{array}{r} 8 \\ \times 2 \\ \hline \end{array}$ 6. $\begin{array}{r} 8 \\ \times 9 \\ \hline \end{array}$

7. $\begin{array}{r} 9 \\ \times 3 \\ \hline \end{array}$ 8. $\begin{array}{r} 8 \\ \times 5 \\ \hline \end{array}$ 9. $\begin{array}{r} 9 \\ \times 2 \\ \hline \end{array}$ 10. $\begin{array}{r} 8 \\ \times 3 \\ \hline \end{array}$ 11. $\begin{array}{r} 7 \\ \times 9 \\ \hline \end{array}$ 12. $\begin{array}{r} 8 \\ \times 7 \\ \hline \end{array}$

13. $\begin{array}{r} 6 \\ \times 9 \\ \hline \end{array}$ 14. $\begin{array}{r} 8 \\ \times 6 \\ \hline \end{array}$ 15. $\begin{array}{r} 9 \\ \times 4 \\ \hline \end{array}$ 16. $\begin{array}{r} 7 \\ \times 8 \\ \hline \end{array}$ 17. $\begin{array}{r} 1 \\ \times 8 \\ \hline \end{array}$ 18. $\begin{array}{r} 9 \\ \times 6 \\ \hline \end{array}$

19. $\begin{array}{r} 3 \\ \times 8 \\ \hline \end{array}$ 20. $\begin{array}{r} 2 \\ \times 9 \\ \hline \end{array}$ 21. $\begin{array}{r} 0 \\ \times 8 \\ \hline \end{array}$ 22. $\begin{array}{r} 4 \\ \times 9 \\ \hline \end{array}$ 23. $\begin{array}{r} 9 \\ \times 9 \\ \hline \end{array}$ 24. $\begin{array}{r} 8 \\ \times 8 \\ \hline \end{array}$

25. $\begin{array}{r} 5 \\ \times 8 \\ \hline \end{array}$ 26. $\begin{array}{r} 0 \\ \times 9 \\ \hline \end{array}$ 27. $\begin{array}{r} 5 \\ \times 9 \\ \hline \end{array}$ 28. $\begin{array}{r} 8 \\ \times 4 \\ \hline \end{array}$ 29. $\begin{array}{r} 3 \\ \times 9 \\ \hline \end{array}$ 30. $\begin{array}{r} 9 \\ \times 9 \\ \hline \end{array}$

31. $\begin{array}{r} 8 \\ \times 9 \\ \hline \end{array}$ 32. $\begin{array}{r} 9 \\ \times 8 \\ \hline \end{array}$ 33. $\begin{array}{r} 1 \\ \times 9 \\ \hline \end{array}$

Multiplication with Factors 6–9

Solve each problem.

Yes, You Can!

1. 4
   ×9

2. 6
   ×8

3. 6
   ×7

4. 8
   ×5

5. 7
   ×6

6. 9
   ×7

7. 2
   ×9

8. 7
   ×7

9. 6
   ×2

10. 8
    ×7

11. 9
    ×8

12. 6
    ×7

13. 8
    ×8

14. 7
    ×8

15. 6
    ×6

16. 2
    ×7

17. 5
    ×9

18. 9
    ×3

19. 1
    ×6

20. 3
    ×8

21. 7
    ×5

22. 4
    ×8

23. 3
    ×6

24. 8
    ×9

25. 4
    ×6

26. 7
    ×4

27. 1
    ×8

28. 5
    ×6

29. 9
    ×9

30. 3
    ×7

31. 9
    ×1

32. 7
    ×9

33. 8
    ×6

Multiplication with Factors 2–9

Solve each problem.

Keep on Marching!

1. 8×5

2. 6×4

3. 5×5

4. 9×5

5. 4×4

6. 6×3

7. 7×4

8. 7×3

9. 3×8

10. 6×2

11. 9×3

12. 5×3

13. 5×4

14. 1×2

15. 5×6

16. 1×4

17. 4×5

18. 2×3

19. 8×2

20. 9×4

21. 4×3

22. 4×2

23. 4×8

24. 7×2

25. 1×5

26. 3×7

27. 3×5

28. 3×4

29. 3×2

30. 2×4

31. 5×2

32. 3×3

33. 9×2

Name _____ Date _____

Multiplication with Factors 2–9

Solve each problem.

Keep Up the Hard Work!

1. 2
  ×7

2. 7
  ×5

3. 5
  ×6

4. 2
  ×7

5. 4
  ×8

6. 7
  ×6

7. 4
  ×9

8. 7
  ×3

9. 6
  ×6

10. 5
  ×9

11. 4
  ×2

12. 2
  ×6

13. 3
  ×6

14. 8
  ×7

15. 8
  ×6

16. 5
  ×7

17. 1
  ×5

18. 4
  ×5

19. 8
  ×5

20. 4
  ×3

21. 6
  ×5

22. 7
  ×7

23. 9
  ×6

24. 7
  ×9

25. 0
  ×6

26. 0
  ×7

27. 5
  ×5

28. 6
  ×7

29. 4
  ×4

30. 6
  ×4

31. 4
  ×7

32. 2
  ×5

33. 1
  ×3

Multiplication with Factors 2–9

Solve each problem.

Dive Deep into Multiplication!

1.   8
   × 7

2.   3
   × 7

3.   6
   × 6

4.   4
   × 7

5.   6
   × 7

6.   6
   × 8

7.   8
   × 8

8.   6
   × 7

9.   5
   × 0

10.   2
   × 8

11.   3
   × 5

12.   3
   × 6

13.   5
   × 5

14.   1
   × 7

15.   7
   × 6

16.   2
   × 7

17.   4
   × 6

18.   9
   × 7

19.   7
   × 7

20.   3
   × 8

21.   5
   × 7

22.   8
   × 6

23.   2
   × 6

24.   4
   × 5

25.   9
   × 8

26.   7
   × 5

27.   8
   × 5

28.   5
   × 5

29.   4
   × 8

30.   7
   × 8

31.   5
   × 9

32.   9
   × 6

33.   5
   × 8

Multiplication with Factors 2–9

Solve each problem.

Slide into Multiplication!

1. 9
   ×4

2. 6
   ×9

3. 5
   ×6

4. 5
   ×3

5. 7
   ×9

6. 8
   ×3

7. 6
   ×7

8. 4
   ×5

9. 4
   ×2

10. 4
    ×4

11. 9
    ×7

12. 8
    ×8

13. 7
    ×2

14. 8
    ×6

15. 6
    ×8

16. 4
    ×6

17. 8
    ×4

18. 6
    ×3

19. 8
    ×5

20. 9
    ×8

21. 4
    ×3

22. 8
    ×9

23. 6
    ×5

24. 9
    ×2

25. 7
    ×4

26. 5
    ×9

27. 5
    ×7

28. 7
    ×3

29. 3
    ×7

30. 7
    ×8

31. 5
    ×7

32. 6
    ×6

33. 8
    ×2

Multiplication with Factors 8–10

Solve each problem. Regroup when necessary.

To the Top!

1. $\begin{array}{r} 8 \\ \times\,5 \\ \hline \end{array}$

2. $\begin{array}{r} 8 \\ \times\,9 \\ \hline \end{array}$

3. $\begin{array}{r} 10 \\ \times\,4 \\ \hline \end{array}$

4. $\begin{array}{r} 9 \\ \times\,9 \\ \hline \end{array}$

5. $\begin{array}{r} 4 \\ \times\,8 \\ \hline \end{array}$

6. $\begin{array}{r} 10 \\ \times\,8 \\ \hline \end{array}$

7. $\begin{array}{r} 10 \\ \times\,10 \\ \hline \end{array}$

8. $\begin{array}{r} 7 \\ \times\,9 \\ \hline \end{array}$

9. $\begin{array}{r} 11 \\ \times\,8 \\ \hline \end{array}$

10. $\begin{array}{r} 9 \\ \times\,8 \\ \hline \end{array}$

11. $\begin{array}{r} 7 \\ \times\,8 \\ \hline \end{array}$

12. $\begin{array}{r} 4 \\ \times\,9 \\ \hline \end{array}$

13. $\begin{array}{r} 3 \\ \times\,8 \\ \hline \end{array}$

14. $\begin{array}{r} 10 \\ \times\,5 \\ \hline \end{array}$

15. $\begin{array}{r} 5 \\ \times\,9 \\ \hline \end{array}$

16. $\begin{array}{r} 3 \\ \times\,9 \\ \hline \end{array}$

17. $\begin{array}{r} 10 \\ \times\,5 \\ \hline \end{array}$

18. $\begin{array}{r} 10 \\ \times\,9 \\ \hline \end{array}$

19. $\begin{array}{r} 12 \\ \times\,8 \\ \hline \end{array}$

20. $\begin{array}{r} 1 \\ \times\,8 \\ \hline \end{array}$

21. $\begin{array}{r} 12 \\ \times\,8 \\ \hline \end{array}$

22. $\begin{array}{r} 10 \\ \times\,7 \\ \hline \end{array}$

23. $\begin{array}{r} 10 \\ \times\,1 \\ \hline \end{array}$

24. $\begin{array}{r} 6 \\ \times\,8 \\ \hline \end{array}$

25. $\begin{array}{r} 10 \\ \times\,9 \\ \hline \end{array}$

26. $\begin{array}{r} 11 \\ \times\,10 \\ \hline \end{array}$

27. $\begin{array}{r} 10 \\ \times\,2 \\ \hline \end{array}$

28. $\begin{array}{r} 12 \\ \times\,9 \\ \hline \end{array}$

29. $\begin{array}{r} 10 \\ \times\,8 \\ \hline \end{array}$

30. $\begin{array}{r} 12 \\ \times\,8 \\ \hline \end{array}$

31. $\begin{array}{r} 9 \\ \times\,1 \\ \hline \end{array}$

32. $\begin{array}{r} 8 \\ \times\,5 \\ \hline \end{array}$

33. $\begin{array}{r} 10 \\ \times\,9 \\ \hline \end{array}$

Multiplication with Factors 11 and 12

Solve each problem. Regroup when necessary.

Climb High with Multiplication!

1. 12 × 7	**2.** 11 × 6	**3.** 12 × 7	**4.** 12 × 6	**5.** 11 × 11	**6.** 11 × 2
7. 11 × 10	**8.** 12 × 9	**9.** 11 × 10	**10.** 12 × 2	**11.** 12 × 10	**12.** 12 × 12
13. 11 × 9	**14.** 12 × 9	**15.** 11 × 8	**16.** 11 × 3	**17.** 11 × 8	**18.** 12 × 10
19. 11 × 9	**20.** 12 × 12	**21.** 12 × 11	**22.** 12 × 1	**23.** 12 × 1	**24.** 12 × 8
25. 12 × 3	**26.** 11 × 7	**27.** 12 × 4	**28.** 12 × 6	**29.** 11 × 9	**30.** 11 × 4
31. 12 × 8	**32.** 11 × 7	**33.** 11 × 5			

Two-Digit by One-Digit Multiplication

Solve each problem.

Fan the Flame of Multiplication!

1. 32
  × 3

2. 23
  × 2

3. 20
  × 4

4. 24
  × 2

5. 44
  × 2

6. 13
  × 3

7. 44
  × 2

8. 22
  × 2

9. 33
  × 3

10. 21
  × 4

11. 21
  × 3

12. 31
  × 3

13. 13
  × 3

14. 31
  × 2

15. 57
  × 1

16. 14
  × 2

17. 30
  × 3

18. 41
  × 2

19. 34
  × 2

20. 21
  × 3

21. 10
  × 7

22. 22
  × 4

23. 33
  × 2

24. 11
  × 4

25. 40
  × 2

26. 43
  × 2

27. 22
  × 4

28. 12
  × 1

29. 12
  × 4

30. 33
  × 2

31. 22
  × 4

32. 11
  × 5

33. 44
  × 2

Two-Digit by One-Digit Multiplication with Regrouping

Solve each problem. Regroup when necessary.

Keep the Fire Going!

1. 16
    × 5

2. 15
    × 7

3. 28
    × 3

4. 24
    × 4

5. 26
    × 4

6. 47
    × 2

7. 19
    × 4

8. 19
    × 5

9. 38
    × 2

10. 45
     × 4

11. 19
     × 6

12. 36
     × 3

13. 14
     × 7

14. 47
     × 2

15. 66
     × 3

16. 53
     × 5

17. 29
     × 4

18. 16
     × 5

19. 23
     × 4

20. 13
     × 6

21. 67
     × 5

22. 14
     × 5

23. 13
     × 7

24. 29
     × 2

25. 32
     × 5

26. 12
     × 8

27. 13
     × 4

28. 35
     × 8

29. 47
     × 3

30. 27
     × 4

31. 28
     × 5

32. 25
     × 3

33. 14
     × 4

Two-Digit by One-Digit Multiplication with Regrouping

Total Problems: **33**
Problems Correct: _____

Solve each problem. Regroup when necessary.

Get to Know Math!

1. $\begin{array}{r} 45 \\ \times\ 2 \\ \hline \end{array}$
   2. $\begin{array}{r} 56 \\ \times\ 4 \\ \hline \end{array}$
   3. $\begin{array}{r} 34 \\ \times\ 3 \\ \hline \end{array}$
   4. $\begin{array}{r} 57 \\ \times\ 4 \\ \hline \end{array}$
   5. $\begin{array}{r} 28 \\ \times\ 3 \\ \hline \end{array}$
   6. $\begin{array}{r} 46 \\ \times\ 6 \\ \hline \end{array}$

7. $\begin{array}{r} 39 \\ \times\ 6 \\ \hline \end{array}$
   8. $\begin{array}{r} 19 \\ \times\ 8 \\ \hline \end{array}$
   9. $\begin{array}{r} 36 \\ \times\ 6 \\ \hline \end{array}$
   10. $\begin{array}{r} 76 \\ \times\ 5 \\ \hline \end{array}$
   11. $\begin{array}{r} 44 \\ \times\ 5 \\ \hline \end{array}$
   12. $\begin{array}{r} 75 \\ \times\ 2 \\ \hline \end{array}$

13. $\begin{array}{r} 27 \\ \times\ 6 \\ \hline \end{array}$
    14. $\begin{array}{r} 22 \\ \times\ 9 \\ \hline \end{array}$
    15. $\begin{array}{r} 83 \\ \times\ 6 \\ \hline \end{array}$
    16. $\begin{array}{r} 87 \\ \times\ 2 \\ \hline \end{array}$
    17. $\begin{array}{r} 37 \\ \times\ 3 \\ \hline \end{array}$
    18. $\begin{array}{r} 49 \\ \times\ 7 \\ \hline \end{array}$

19. $\begin{array}{r} 74 \\ \times\ 3 \\ \hline \end{array}$
    20. $\begin{array}{r} 37 \\ \times\ 6 \\ \hline \end{array}$
    21. $\begin{array}{r} 53 \\ \times\ 5 \\ \hline \end{array}$
    22. $\begin{array}{r} 68 \\ \times\ 4 \\ \hline \end{array}$
    23. $\begin{array}{r} 38 \\ \times\ 4 \\ \hline \end{array}$
    24. $\begin{array}{r} 77 \\ \times\ 8 \\ \hline \end{array}$

25. $\begin{array}{r} 63 \\ \times\ 7 \\ \hline \end{array}$
    26. $\begin{array}{r} 59 \\ \times\ 4 \\ \hline \end{array}$
    27. $\begin{array}{r} 42 \\ \times\ 7 \\ \hline \end{array}$
    28. $\begin{array}{r} 55 \\ \times\ 3 \\ \hline \end{array}$
    29. $\begin{array}{r} 57 \\ \times\ 3 \\ \hline \end{array}$
    30. $\begin{array}{r} 69 \\ \times\ 2 \\ \hline \end{array}$

31. $\begin{array}{r} 59 \\ \times\ 2 \\ \hline \end{array}$
    32. $\begin{array}{r} 22 \\ \times\ 8 \\ \hline \end{array}$
    33. $\begin{array}{r} 57 \\ \times\ 8 \\ \hline \end{array}$

Two-Digit by One-Digit Multiplication with Regrouping

Total Problems:	**33**
Problems Correct:	_____

Solve each problem. Regroup when necessary.

Math Is Your Friend!

1. 34
    × 3

2. 35
    × 3

3. 13
    × 5

4. 26
    × 3

5. 15
    × 3

6. 28
    × 4

7. 36
    × 2

8. 24
    × 3

9. 15
    × 7

10. 26
    × 3

11. 17
    × 7

12. 28
    × 3

13. 36
    × 3

14. 25
    × 4

15. 14
    × 7

16. 13
    × 7

17. 35
    × 2

18. 19
    × 5

19. 14
    × 5

20. 17
    × 6

21. 15
    × 6

22. 36
    × 6

23. 15
    × 3

24. 18
    × 7

25. 12
    × 6

26. 28
    × 4

27. 37
    × 3

28. 24
    × 4

29. 33
    × 4

30. 44
    × 3

31. 23
    × 4

32. 35
    × 3

33. 28
    × 2

Two-Digit by One-Digit Multiplication with Regrouping

Solve each problem. Regroup when necessary.

Discover Multiplication!

1. 58
   $\times$ 6

2. 82
   $\times$ 6

3. 32
   $\times$ 7

4. 27
   $\times$ 6

5. 45
   $\times$ 2

6. 28
   $\times$ 5

7. 66
   $\times$ 7

8. 83
   $\times$ 5

9. 77
   $\times$ 8

10. 57
   $\times$ 8

11. 43
   $\times$ 9

12. 86
   $\times$ 5

13. 74
   $\times$ 7

14. 69
   $\times$ 2

15. 28
   $\times$ 4

16. 54
   $\times$ 7

17. 64
   $\times$ 7

18. 36
   $\times$ 6

19. 42
   $\times$ 3

20. 54
   $\times$ 4

21. 63
   $\times$ 6

22. 87
   $\times$ 2

23. 46
   $\times$ 7

24. 49
   $\times$ 5

25. 36
   $\times$ 2

26. 38
   $\times$ 9

27. 44
   $\times$ 3

28. 55
   $\times$ 4

29. 33
   $\times$ 8

30. 87
   $\times$ 3

31. 47
   $\times$ 4

32. 78
   $\times$ 2

33. 65
   $\times$ 5

Two-Digit by One-Digit Multiplication with Regrouping

Solve each problem. Regroup when necessary.

Explore Multiplication!

1. 78
   × 2

2. 65
   × 2

3. 68
   × 2

4. 36
   × 4

5. 43
   × 5

6. 59
   × 2

7. 46
   × 5

8. 63
   × 5

9. 55
   × 2

10. 48
    × 7

11. 49
    × 8

12. 64
    × 7

13. 67
    × 3

14. 47
    × 4

15. 39
    × 4

16. 82
    × 6

17. 73
    × 4

18. 37
    × 4

19. 27
    × 5

20. 36
    × 4

21. 57
    × 2

22. 74
    × 8

23. 68
    × 2

24. 58
    × 3

25. 64
    × 6

26. 37
    × 5

27. 46
    × 5

28. 48
    × 5

29. 77
    × 4

30. 44
    × 8

31. 83
    × 5

32. 48
    × 4

33. 75
    × 2

Two-Digit by One-Digit Multiplication with Regrouping

Solve each problem. Regroup when necessary.

Three Cheers for Multiplication!

1.	2.	3.	4.	5.	6.
57	58	73	17	97	68
× 7	× 2	× 4	× 6	× 2	× 3

7.	8.	9.	10.	11.	12.
63	66	18	65	49	73
× 5	× 2	× 9	× 5	× 5	× 5

13.	14.	15.	16.	17.	18.
59	39	44	78	48	58
× 3	× 2	× 4	× 6	× 6	× 8

19.	20.	21.	22.	23.	24.
85	99	55	84	49	69
× 4	× 4	× 2	× 4	× 5	× 3

25.	26.	27.	28.	29.	30.
88	46	48	89	74	14
× 8	× 3	× 3	× 3	× 4	× 3

31.	32.	33.
42	78	49
× 7	× 8	× 7

Name _____   Date _____

Three-Digit by One-Digit Multiplication with Regrouping

Solve each problem. Regroup when necessary.

Hooray for Math!

1. 124
    × 7

2. 813
    × 8

3. 379
    × 8

4. 288
    × 5

5. 585
    × 2

6. 703
    × 4

7. 956
    × 2

8. 486
    × 9

9. 377
    × 3

10. 496
    × 3

11. 778
    × 2

12. 539
    × 3

13. 453
    × 2

14. 535
    × 6

15. 848
    × 5

16. 818
    × 3

17. 524
    × 6

18. 772
    × 5

19. 745
    × 3

20. 836
    × 2

21. 734
    × 2

22. 676
    × 5

23. 517
    × 7

24. 845
    × 3

25. 784
    × 4

26. 964
    × 3

27. 634
    × 4

28. 756
    × 3

29. 516
    × 6

30. 634
    × 2

31. 529
    × 8

32. 584
    × 4

33. 291
    × 2

Three-Digit by One-Digit Multiplication

Solve each problem. Regroup when necessary.

Think Big!

1. 365×2	**2.** 524×6	**3.** 669×8	**4.** 437×6	**5.** 465×2	**6.** 594×3
7. 608×9	**8.** 548×5	**9.** 623×7	**10.** 589×4	**11.** 336×4	**12.** 121×5
13. 237×3	**14.** 992×9	**15.** 652×5	**16.** 327×6	**17.** 776×7	**18.** 733×3
19. 532×6	**20.** 762×5	**21.** 259×3	**22.** 476×8	**23.** 649×3	**24.** 324×7
25. 122×8	**26.** 231×3	**27.** 782×6	**28.** 769×5	**29.** 898×5	**30.** 688×2
31. 353×5	**32.** 984×6	**33.** 362×7			

CD-104320 • © Carson-Dellosa

Four-Digit by One-Digit Multiplication with Regrouping

Solve each problem. Regroup when necessary.

A Whale of a Job!

1. 3,237
    × 8

2. 4,348
    × 9

3. 8,900
    × 8

4. 6,908
    × 4

5. 7,934
    × 3

6. 6,343
    × 7

7. 3,498
    × 7

8. 9,980
    × 5

9. 7,914
    × 7

10. 6,756
     × 9

11. 7,234
     × 3

12. 4,348
     × 5

13. 6,743
     × 3

14. 5,967
     × 3

15. 4,987
     × 2

16. 8,554
     × 2

17. 2,393
     × 4

18. 6,374
     × 2

19. 7,834
     × 2

20. 2,045
     × 2

21. 7,984
     × 3

22. 2,494
     × 4

23. 8,021
     × 5

24. 7,498
     × 3

25. 3,946
     × 7

26. 7,145
     × 5

27. 6,945
     × 5

28. 4,392
     × 3

29. 3,234
     × 2

30. 5,127
     × 6

31. 8,483
     × 4

32. 8,612
     × 6

33. 6,947
     × 5

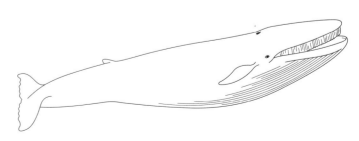

Four-Digit by One-Digit Multiplication with Regrouping

Total Problems: **33**
Problems Correct: _____

Solve each problem. Regroup when necessary.

Let's See Your Smile!

1. 4,113 × 6	**2.** 7,312 × 7	**3.** 8,900 × 8	**4.** 5,308 × 4	**5.** 4,930 × 4	**6.** 6,342 × 5
7. 4,213 × 6	**8.** 9,980 × 5	**9.** 2,794 × 7	**10.** 9,755 × 8	**11.** 3,214 × 7	**12.** 2,317 × 3
13. 6,746 × 3	**14.** 6,677 × 4	**15.** 8,227 × 2	**16.** 5,857 × 3	**17.** 3,351 × 5	**18.** 2,356 × 3
19. 4,845 × 2	**20.** 7,934 × 3	**21.** 4,065 × 6	**22.** 2,132 × 6	**23.** 7,021 × 4	**24.** 9,442 × 3
25. 4,365 × 6	**26.** 3,225 × 5	**27.** 8,222 × 4	**28.** 7,422 × 5	**29.** 8,265 × 3	**30.** 7,120 × 2
31. 7,322 × 6	**32.** 6,434 × 6	**33.** 7,387 × 5			

Two-Digit by Two-Digit Multiplication with Regrouping

Solve each problem. Regroup when necessary.

Keep Your Eye on the Ball!

1. 48
×38

2. 63
×73

3. 67
×24

4. 89
×24

5. 55
×63

6. 39
×28

7. 51
×40

8. 48
×69

9. 58
×73

10. 73
×28

11. 55
×33

12. 88
×62

13. 34
×66

14. 62
×44

15. 68
×59

16. 27
×45

17. 29
×89

18. 53
×24

19. 28
×48

20. 70
×47

21. 50
×42

22. 38
×22

23. 45
×56

24. 62
×46

25. 76
×49

26. 66
×38

27. 37
×48

28. 67
×49

29. 67
×81

30. 47
×86

31. 48
×29

32. 45
×28

33. 32
×62

Two-Digit by Two-Digit Multiplication with Regrouping

Total Problems: **27**
Problems Correct: _____

Solve each problem. Regroup when necessary.

See the Fruit of Your Hard Work!

1. $\begin{array}{r} 58 \\ \times\,26 \\ \hline \end{array}$
2. $\begin{array}{r} 74 \\ \times\,49 \\ \hline \end{array}$
3. $\begin{array}{r} 69 \\ \times\,27 \\ \hline \end{array}$
4. $\begin{array}{r} 57 \\ \times\,44 \\ \hline \end{array}$
5. $\begin{array}{r} 44 \\ \times\,37 \\ \hline \end{array}$
6. $\begin{array}{r} 28 \\ \times\,37 \\ \hline \end{array}$

7. $\begin{array}{r} 45 \\ \times\,36 \\ \hline \end{array}$
8. $\begin{array}{r} 32 \\ \times\,49 \\ \hline \end{array}$
9. $\begin{array}{r} 59 \\ \times\,30 \\ \hline \end{array}$
10. $\begin{array}{r} 67 \\ \times\,85 \\ \hline \end{array}$
11. $\begin{array}{r} 52 \\ \times\,47 \\ \hline \end{array}$
12. $\begin{array}{r} 54 \\ \times\,72 \\ \hline \end{array}$

13. $\begin{array}{r} 63 \\ \times\,41 \\ \hline \end{array}$
14. $\begin{array}{r} 73 \\ \times\,55 \\ \hline \end{array}$
15. $\begin{array}{r} 36 \\ \times\,27 \\ \hline \end{array}$
16. $\begin{array}{r} 61 \\ \times\,72 \\ \hline \end{array}$
17. $\begin{array}{r} 37 \\ \times\,51 \\ \hline \end{array}$
18. $\begin{array}{r} 68 \\ \times\,52 \\ \hline \end{array}$

19. $\begin{array}{r} 79 \\ \times\,22 \\ \hline \end{array}$
20. $\begin{array}{r} 48 \\ \times\,62 \\ \hline \end{array}$
21. $\begin{array}{r} 94 \\ \times\,38 \\ \hline \end{array}$
22. $\begin{array}{r} 46 \\ \times\,79 \\ \hline \end{array}$
23. $\begin{array}{r} 67 \\ \times\,38 \\ \hline \end{array}$
24. $\begin{array}{r} 63 \\ \times\,39 \\ \hline \end{array}$

25. $\begin{array}{r} 66 \\ \times\,29 \\ \hline \end{array}$
26. $\begin{array}{r} 51 \\ \times\,26 \\ \hline \end{array}$
27. $\begin{array}{r} 65 \\ \times\,24 \\ \hline \end{array}$

Three-Digit by Two-Digit Multiplication with Regrouping

Total Problems: **27**
Problems Correct: _____

Solve each problem. Regroup when necessary.

Take a Bite Out of Multiplication!

1. 486
 × 22

2. 212
 × 56

3. 333
 × 37

4. 667
 × 39

5. 795
 × 48

6. 583
 × 26

7. 402
 × 19

8. 779
 × 31

9. 376
 × 55

10. 433
 × 63

11. 560
 × 35

12. 731
 × 25

13. 324
 × 25

14. 254
 × 87

15. 107
 × 45

16. 204
 × 91

17. 658
 × 87

18. 547
 × 34

19. 232
 × 15

20. 730
 × 32

21. 477
 × 20

22. 720
 × 37

23. 589
 × 27

24. 526
 × 32

25. 896
 × 25

26. 218
 × 13

27. 539
 × 22

Three-Digit by Two-Digit Multiplication with Regrouping

Solve each problem. Regroup when necessary.

Multiplication Is a Hoot!

1. 732 × 28	**2.** 523 × 84	**3.** 745 × 22	**4.** 670 × 54	**5.** 634 × 99	**6.** 246 × 51
7. 222 × 37	**8.** 208 × 40	**9.** 538 × 88	**10.** 798 × 55	**11.** 750 × 58	**12.** 162 × 32
13. 830 × 65	**14.** 727 × 42	**15.** 233 × 28	**16.** 499 × 21	**17.** 292 × 68	**18.** 740 × 45
19. 896 × 35	**20.** 634 × 32	**21.** 769 × 42	**22.** 621 × 44	**23.** 283 × 30	**24.** 427 × 40
25. 285 × 46	**26.** 342 × 33	**27.** 648 × 32			

CD-104320 • © Carson-Dellosa

Three-Digit by Three-Digit Multiplication with Regrouping

Total Problems: **27**
Problems Correct: _____

Solve each problem. Regroup when necessary.

Who-oo Likes to Multiply?

1. 325
    × 432

2. 265
    × 679

3. 721
    × 428

4. 236
    × 265

5. 123
    × 245

6. 248
    × 693

7. 343
    × 675

8. 649
    × 394

9. 476
    × 285

10. 438
    × 549

11. 845
    × 723

12. 722
    × 386

13. 434
    × 434

14. 365
    × 342

15. 362
    × 694

16. 998
    × 367

17. 554
    × 872

18. 351
    × 523

19. 569
    × 438

20. 460
    × 126

21. 659
    × 532

22. 448
    × 749

23. 538
    × 345

24. 477
    × 361

25. 258
    × 439

26. 453
    × 850

27. 241
    × 231

Multiplication of Decimals

Solve each problem. Regroup when necessary.

Total Problems: **33**
Problems Correct: _____

Thumbs Up for Math!

1. $\begin{array}{r} 3.65 \\ \times\ \ 2 \\ \hline \end{array}$

2. $\begin{array}{r} 5.24 \\ \times\ \ 6 \\ \hline \end{array}$

3. $\begin{array}{r} 6.69 \\ \times\ \ 8 \\ \hline \end{array}$

4. $\begin{array}{r} 4.37 \\ \times\ \ 6 \\ \hline \end{array}$

5. $\begin{array}{r} 4.65 \\ \times\ \ 2 \\ \hline \end{array}$

6. $\begin{array}{r} 5.94 \\ \times\ \ 3 \\ \hline \end{array}$

7. $\begin{array}{r} 6.08 \\ \times\ \ 9 \\ \hline \end{array}$

8. $\begin{array}{r} 5.48 \\ \times\ \ 5 \\ \hline \end{array}$

9. $\begin{array}{r} 6.23 \\ \times\ \ 7 \\ \hline \end{array}$

10. $\begin{array}{r} 5.89 \\ \times\ \ 4 \\ \hline \end{array}$

11. $\begin{array}{r} 3.36 \\ \times\ \ 4 \\ \hline \end{array}$

12. $\begin{array}{r} 1.24 \\ \times\ \ 5 \\ \hline \end{array}$

13. $\begin{array}{r} 2.37 \\ \times\ \ 3 \\ \hline \end{array}$

14. $\begin{array}{r} 9.92 \\ \times\ \ 9 \\ \hline \end{array}$

15. $\begin{array}{r} 6.52 \\ \times\ \ 5 \\ \hline \end{array}$

16. $\begin{array}{r} 3.27 \\ \times\ \ 6 \\ \hline \end{array}$

17. $\begin{array}{r} 7.76 \\ \times\ \ 7 \\ \hline \end{array}$

18. $\begin{array}{r} 7.33 \\ \times\ \ 3 \\ \hline \end{array}$

19. $\begin{array}{r} 5.32 \\ \times\ \ 6 \\ \hline \end{array}$

20. $\begin{array}{r} 7.62 \\ \times\ \ 5 \\ \hline \end{array}$

21. $\begin{array}{r} 2.59 \\ \times\ \ 3 \\ \hline \end{array}$

22. $\begin{array}{r} 4.76 \\ \times\ \ 8 \\ \hline \end{array}$

23. $\begin{array}{r} 6.49 \\ \times\ \ 8 \\ \hline \end{array}$

24. $\begin{array}{r} 3.24 \\ \times\ \ 7 \\ \hline \end{array}$

25. $\begin{array}{r} 1.22 \\ \times\ \ 8 \\ \hline \end{array}$

26. $\begin{array}{r} 2.31 \\ \times\ \ 3 \\ \hline \end{array}$

27. $\begin{array}{r} 7.82 \\ \times\ \ 6 \\ \hline \end{array}$

28. $\begin{array}{r} 7.69 \\ \times\ \ 5 \\ \hline \end{array}$

29. $\begin{array}{r} 8.98 \\ \times\ \ 5 \\ \hline \end{array}$

30. $\begin{array}{r} 6.88 \\ \times\ \ 2 \\ \hline \end{array}$

31. $\begin{array}{r} 3.53 \\ \times\ \ 5 \\ \hline \end{array}$

32. $\begin{array}{r} 9.84 \\ \times\ \ 6 \\ \hline \end{array}$

33. $\begin{array}{r} 3.62 \\ \times\ \ 7 \\ \hline \end{array}$

Multiplication of Decimals

Solve each problem. Regroup when necessary.

You're Doing Great!

1. 41.13
× 6

2. 73.12
× 7

3. 89.00
× 8

4. 53.08
× 4

5. 49.30
× 4

6. 63.42
× 5

7. 42.13
× 6

8. 99.80
× 5

9. 27.94
× 7

10. 97.55
× 8

11. 32.14
× 7

12. 23.17
× 3

13. 67.43
× 8

14. 66.67
× 4

15. 82.27
× 2

16. 57.72
× 3

17. 63.51
× 5

18. 53.34
× 8

19. 23.23
× 3

20. 48.45
× 2

21. 79.34
× 3

22. 21.32
× 6

23. 70.21
× 4

24. 94.42
× 3

25. 43.65
× 6

26. 32.25
× 5

27. 82.22
× 4

28. 74.22
× 5

29. 82.65
× 3

30. 71.20
× 2

31. 73.22
× 6

32. 64.34
× 6

33. 73.87
× 5

Name _____ Date _____

Multiplication of Decimals

Solve each problem. Regroup when necessary.

You're Number One!

1. 3.65
   × 2

2. 5.24
   × 6

3. 6.69
   × 8

4. 4.37
   × 6

5. 4.65
   × 2

6. 5.94
   × 3

7. 6.08
   × 9

8. 5.48
   × 5

9. 6.23
   × 7

10. 5.89
    × 4

11. 3.36
    × 4

12. 1.24
    × 5

13. 2.37
    × 3

14. 9.92
    × 9

15. 6.52
    × 5

16. 3.27
    × 6

17. 7.76
    × 7

18. 7.33
    × 3

19. 5.32
    × 6

20. 7.62
    × 5

21. 2.59
    × 3

22. 4.76
    × 8

23. 6.49
    × 3

24. 3.24
    × 7

25. 1.22
    × 8

26. 2.31
    × 3

27. 7.82
    × 6

28. 7.69
    × 5

29. 8.98
    × 5

30. 6.88
    × 2

31. 3.53
    × 5

32. 9.84
    × 6

33. 3.62
    × 7

Multiplication of Decimals

Total Problems: **33**
Problems Correct: _____

Solve each problem. Regroup when necessary.

Go for the Gold!

1. 25.72
    ×   8

2. 33.55
    ×   6

3. 76.28
    ×   3

4. 97.65
    ×   2

5. 67.90
    ×   3

6. 38.67
    ×   6

7. 80.07
    ×   9

8. 82.15
    ×   7

9. 22.52
    ×   8

10. 25.86
    ×   2

11. 76.39
    ×   2

12. 21.22
    ×   5

13. 61.56
    ×   6

14. 73.85
    ×   9

15. 23.25
    ×   6

16. 82.52
    ×   9

17. 20.99
    ×   8

18. 62.87
    ×   9

19. 30.59
    ×   2

20. 61.93
    ×   6

21. 97.12
    ×   8

22. 56.19
    ×   3

23. 58.16
    ×   3

24. 36.87
    ×   9

25. 98.20
    ×   7

26. 29.19
    ×   8

27. 70.62
    ×   3

28. 88.38
    ×   5

29. 35.56
    ×   2

30. 98.72
    ×   7

31. 35.62
    ×   2

32. 27.00
    ×   7

33. 29.92
    ×   7

Division with One-Digit Quotients

Solve each problem.

Surf Through Division!

1. $4\overline{)36}$

2. $5\overline{)20}$

3. $7\overline{)21}$

4. $6\overline{)24}$

5. $7\overline{)42}$

6. $4\overline{)16}$

7. $5\overline{)35}$

8. $3\overline{)21}$

9. $9\overline{)63}$

10. $9\overline{)45}$

11. $8\overline{)48}$

12. $6\overline{)12}$

13. $6\overline{)42}$

14. $7\overline{)56}$

15. $9\overline{)54}$

16. $5\overline{)35}$

17. $6\overline{)30}$

18. $3\overline{)9}$

19. $7\overline{)63}$

20. $8\overline{)32}$

21. $6\overline{)30}$

22. $4\overline{)28}$

23. $9\overline{)36}$

24. $8\overline{)16}$

25. $5\overline{)45}$

26. $4\overline{)20}$

27. $7\overline{)49}$

28. $9\overline{)36}$

29. $8\overline{)64}$

30. $9\overline{)18}$

31. $6\overline{)48}$

32. $6\overline{)54}$

33. $8\overline{)56}$

34. $4\overline{)32}$

35. $3\overline{)24}$

36. $2\overline{)14}$

Division with One-Digit Quotients

Solve each problem.

Make Waves with Division!

1. $5\overline{)35}$ **2.** $9\overline{)36}$ **3.** $7\overline{)21}$ **4.** $9\overline{)27}$

5. $4\overline{)12}$ **6.** $4\overline{)16}$ **7.** $9\overline{)18}$ **8.** $6\overline{)30}$

9. $1\overline{)5}$ **10.** $5\overline{)30}$ **11.** $5\overline{)40}$ **12.** $9\overline{)27}$

13. $3\overline{)18}$ **14.** $7\overline{)28}$ **15.** $3\overline{)24}$ **16.** $4\overline{)32}$

17. $3\overline{)21}$ **18.** $5\overline{)25}$ **19.** $5\overline{)15}$ **20.** $1\overline{)9}$

21. $3\overline{)27}$ **22.** $8\overline{)64}$ **23.** $6\overline{)24}$ **24.** $6\overline{)36}$

25. $8\overline{)32}$ **26.** $4\overline{)36}$ **27.** $8\overline{)24}$ **28.** $7\overline{)14}$

29. $2\overline{)18}$ **30.** $8\overline{)8}$ **31.** $4\overline{)24}$ **32.** $5\overline{)20}$

33. $8\overline{)16}$ **34.** $5\overline{)5}$ **35.** $3\overline{)15}$ **36.** $7\overline{)49}$

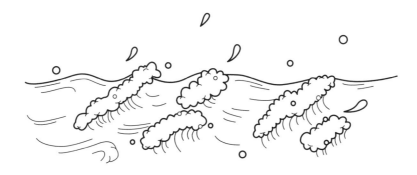

Division with One-Digit Quotients

Solve each problem.

Float Through Division!

1. $4\overline{)20}$

2. $5\overline{)20}$

3. $7\overline{)28}$

4. $9\overline{)54}$

5. $6\overline{)36}$

6. $9\overline{)54}$

7. $5\overline{)45}$

8. $5\overline{)30}$

9. $8\overline{)56}$

10. $6\overline{)42}$

11. $4\overline{)36}$

12. $4\overline{)32}$

13. $7\overline{)56}$

14. $6\overline{)54}$

15. $4\overline{)28}$

16. $8\overline{)32}$

17. $8\overline{)48}$

18. $5\overline{)35}$

19. $4\overline{)24}$

20. $7\overline{)21}$

21. $6\overline{)30}$

22. $9\overline{)45}$

23. $9\overline{)90}$

24. $7\overline{)49}$

25. $6\overline{)48}$

26. $7\overline{)35}$

27. $7\overline{)42}$

28. $4\overline{)36}$

29. $8\overline{)56}$

30. $8\overline{)64}$

31. $5\overline{)40}$

32. $3\overline{)21}$

33. $9\overline{)63}$

34. $7\overline{)63}$

35. $7\overline{)28}$

36. $4\overline{)32}$

CD-104320 • © Carson-Dellosa

Name _____ Date _____

Division with One-Digit Quotients

Solve each problem.

Division Is Smooth Sailing!

1. 8)64   2. 9)81   3. 7)28   4. 7)49

5. 8)16   6. 1)4   7. 9)45   8. 7)35

9. 4)12   10. 8)72   11. 6)42   12. 5)45

13. 6)54   14. 3)27   15. 8)40   16. 9)36

17. 9)81   18. 4)20   19. 7)56   20. 6)30

21. 6)42   22. 5)15   23. 4)24   24. 6)54

25. 5)30   26. 4)36   27. 2)18   28. 4)36

29. 3)27   30. 9)9   31. 3)24   32. 4)32

33. 3)9   34. 8)56   35. 4)36   36. 8)32

Division with One-Digit Quotients

Solve each problem.

Beautiful Work!

1. $6\overline{)48}$ **2.** $3\overline{)27}$ **3.** $4\overline{)20}$ **4.** $7\overline{)49}$

5. $5\overline{)45}$ **6.** $7\overline{)42}$ **7.** $8\overline{)32}$ **8.** $7\overline{)35}$

9. $3\overline{)18}$ **10.** $9\overline{)72}$ **11.** $8\overline{)56}$ **12.** $8\overline{)48}$

13. $7\overline{)28}$ **14.** $7\overline{)7}$ **15.** $3\overline{)24}$ **16.** $8\overline{)72}$

17. $6\overline{)24}$ **18.** $4\overline{)32}$ **19.** $9\overline{)54}$ **20.** $9\overline{)9}$

21. $8\overline{)40}$ **22.** $4\overline{)28}$ **23.** $8\overline{)48}$ **24.** $3\overline{)6}$

25. $5\overline{)35}$ **26.** $1\overline{)4}$ **27.** $8\overline{)64}$ **28.** $4\overline{)32}$

29. $5\overline{)25}$ **30.** $5\overline{)40}$ **31.** $7\overline{)42}$ **32.** $9\overline{)81}$

33. $6\overline{)54}$ **34.** $3\overline{)21}$ **35.** $8\overline{)56}$ **36.** $6\overline{)18}$

Name _____ Date _____

Division with One-Digit Quotients

Total Problems: **36**
Problems Correct: _____

Solve each problem.

Now You're Flying!

1. $5\overline{)45}$ **2.** $8\overline{)56}$ **3.** $5\overline{)40}$ **4.** $1\overline{)9}$

5. $6\overline{)36}$ **6.** $8\overline{)32}$ **7.** $8\overline{)72}$ **8.** $8\overline{)8}$

9. $7\overline{)63}$ **10.** $9\overline{)27}$ **11.** $3\overline{)27}$ **12.** $4\overline{)36}$

13. $3\overline{)12}$ **14.** $3\overline{)21}$ **15.** $6\overline{)30}$ **16.** $9\overline{)54}$

17. $4\overline{)24}$ **18.** $1\overline{)7}$ **19.** $5\overline{)45}$ **20.** $9\overline{)72}$

21. $7\overline{)42}$ **22.** $7\overline{)28}$ **23.** $7\overline{)56}$ **24.** $5\overline{)35}$

25. $9\overline{)54}$ **26.** $7\overline{)49}$ **27.** $2\overline{)16}$ **28.** $3\overline{)24}$

29. $2\overline{)14}$ **30.** $9\overline{)63}$ **31.** $4\overline{)32}$ **32.** $6\overline{)54}$

33. $8\overline{)64}$ **34.** $8\overline{)24}$ **35.** $6\overline{)42}$ **36.** $4\overline{)28}$

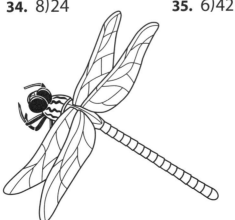

Name _____ Date _____

Division with One-Digit Quotients and Remainders

Solve each problem.

Total Problems: **30**
Problems Correct: _____

Jump into Division!

1. $8\overline{)37}$ **2.** $6\overline{)34}$ **3.** $2\overline{)15}$

4. $7\overline{)37}$ **5.** $7\overline{)23}$ **6.** $3\overline{)28}$

7. $5\overline{)27}$ **8.** $9\overline{)28}$ **9.** $6\overline{)35}$

10. $3\overline{)22}$ **11.** $4\overline{)30}$ **12.** $4\overline{)21}$

13. $9\overline{)44}$ **14.** $5\overline{)21}$ **15.** $7\overline{)26}$

16. $9\overline{)38}$ **17.** $8\overline{)27}$ **18.** $3\overline{)22}$

19. $7\overline{)15}$ **20.** $7\overline{)48}$ **21.** $8\overline{)42}$

22. $3\overline{)25}$ **23.** $8\overline{)34}$ **24.** $6\overline{)17}$

25. $5\overline{)47}$ **26.** $7\overline{)27}$ **27.** $6\overline{)21}$

28. $9\overline{)32}$ **29.** $4\overline{)26}$ **30.** $6\overline{)22}$

CD-104320 • © Carson-Dellosa

Name _____   Date _____

Division with One-Digit Quotients and Remainders

Solve each problem.

Hop to It!

1. 6)32

2. 8)41

3. 4)29

4. 7)64

5. 8)57

6. 7)37

7. 9)65

8. 7)30

9. 9)74

10. 6)44

11. 6)50

12. 9)56

13. 5)34

14. 7)53

15. 7)45

16. 5)8

17. 9)47

18. 4)37

19. 9)38

20. 5)36

21. 9)33

22. 8)49

23. 5)42

24. 7)58

25. 5)46

26. 8)73

27. 6)57

28. 7)40

29. 8)65

30. 5)34

Division with One-Digit Quotients and Remainders

Total Problems: **30**
Problems Correct: _____

Solve each problem.

Think Big!

1. $9\overline{)65}$

2. $2\overline{)17}$

3. $5\overline{)32}$

4. $3\overline{)26}$

5. $8\overline{)65}$

6. $3\overline{)19}$

7. $6\overline{)34}$

8. $8\overline{)79}$

9. $5\overline{)16}$

10. $2\overline{)17}$

11. $2\overline{)5}$

12. $7\overline{)43}$

13. $7\overline{)57}$

14. $5\overline{)21}$

15. $7\overline{)68}$

16. $4\overline{)39}$

17. $8\overline{)38}$

18. $5\overline{)49}$

19. $6\overline{)51}$

20. $8\overline{)41}$

21. $5\overline{)27}$

22. $7\overline{)22}$

23. $8\overline{)73}$

24. $6\overline{)47}$

25. $6\overline{)34}$

26. $3\overline{)25}$

27. $6\overline{)23}$

28. $4\overline{)17}$

29. $5\overline{)21}$

30. $9\overline{)51}$

Division with One-Digit Quotients and Remainders

Solve each problem.

Sink Your Teeth into Division!

1. 3)19   **2.** 7)48   **3.** 5)29

4. 7)43   **5.** 7)23   **6.** 4)31

7. 4)6   **8.** 7)39   **9.** 5)26

10. 8)30   **11.** 6)39   **12.** 9)26

13. 8)50   **14.** 9)47   **15.** 8)75

16. 9)38   **17.** 7)22   **18.** 6)47

19. 5)26   **20.** 5)34   **21.** 6)51

22. 8)53   **23.** 5)29   **24.** 9)62

25. 7)36   **26.** 7)50   **27.** 9)66

28. 3)28   **29.** 7)34   **30.** 3)22

Name _____ Date _____

Division with One-Digit Quotients and Remainders

Solve each problem.

You're Doing an Egg-cellent Job!

1. $8\overline{)70}$

2. $4\overline{)27}$

3. $2\overline{)13}$

4. $3\overline{)16}$

5. $6\overline{)21}$

6. $5\overline{)31}$

7. $9\overline{)48}$

8. $7\overline{)45}$

9. $8\overline{)46}$

10. $9\overline{)39}$

11. $6\overline{)49}$

12. $8\overline{)66}$

13. $9\overline{)74}$

14. $6\overline{)32}$

15. $2\overline{)15}$

16. $3\overline{)19}$

17. $7\overline{)41}$

18. $5\overline{)48}$

19. $5\overline{)44}$

20. $7\overline{)30}$

21. $9\overline{)51}$

22. $4\overline{)26}$

23. $6\overline{)43}$

24. $9\overline{)77}$

25. $8\overline{)39}$

26. $7\overline{)60}$

27. $4\overline{)37}$

28. $7\overline{)68}$

29. $3\overline{)29}$

30. $4\overline{)35}$

Name _____ Date _____

Division with Two-Digit Quotients

Total Problems: **36**
Problems Correct: _____

Solve each problem.

Get Cracking!

1. 2)84   **2.** 9)99   **3.** 2)24   **4.** 2)46

5. 6)66   **6.** 2)66   **7.** 3)69   **8.** 2)62

9. 8)88   **10.** 4)84   **11.** 3)33   **12.** 9)90

13. 2)68   **14.** 5)50   **15.** 6)60   **16.** 8)88

17. 2)64   **18.** 3)93   **19.** 3)63   **20.** 7)77

21. 7)70   **22.** 3)96   **23.** 3)69   **24.** 2)86

25. 4)48   **26.** 2)68   **27.** 2)26   **28.** 4)48

29. 2)84   **30.** 2)66   **31.** 2)22   **32.** 1)11

33. 5)55   **34.** 5)50   **35.** 3)39   **36.** 7)77

Division with Two-Digit Quotients

Solve each problem.

Get a Taste of Division!

1. $2\overline{)84}$ **2.** $2\overline{)62}$ **3.** $2\overline{)68}$ **4.** $3\overline{)93}$

5. $7\overline{)70}$ **6.** $5\overline{)55}$ **7.** $3\overline{)69}$ **8.** $9\overline{)99}$

9. $3\overline{)36}$ **10.** $9\overline{)90}$ **11.** $2\overline{)46}$ **12.** $2\overline{)26}$

13. $2\overline{)64}$ **14.** $7\overline{)77}$ **15.** $3\overline{)99}$ **16.** $2\overline{)24}$

17. $4\overline{)84}$ **18.** $8\overline{)88}$ **19.** $3\overline{)63}$ **20.** $5\overline{)50}$

21. $2\overline{)48}$ **22.** $2\overline{)28}$ **23.** $8\overline{)88}$ **24.** $7\overline{)70}$

25. $4\overline{)48}$ **26.** $2\overline{)66}$ **27.** $2\overline{)86}$ **28.** $1\overline{)63}$

29. $4\overline{)44}$ **30.** $4\overline{)80}$ **31.** $6\overline{)60}$ **32.** $3\overline{)39}$

33. $3\overline{)96}$ **34.** $8\overline{)80}$ **35.** $2\overline{)82}$ **36.** $2\overline{)86}$

Name _____   Date _____

Division with Two-Digit Quotients

Solve each problem.

Division Is a Piece of Cake!

1. 7)455   **2.** 3)201   **3.** 7)616   **4.** 3)225

5. 8)744   **6.** 5)405   **7.** 6)348   **8.** 4)216

9. 6)324   **10.** 2)176   **11.** 5)270   **12.** 7)644

13. 2)194   **14.** 6)378   **15.** 2)138   **16.** 3)282

17. 9)252   **18.** 8)120   **19.** 8)504   **20.** 9)855

21. 3)225   **22.** 9)225   **23.** 3)171   **24.** 3)102

25. 4)224   **26.** 5)435   **27.** 4)304   **28.** 5)455

29. 2)148   **30.** 7)455   **31.** 9)306   **32.** 6)588

33. 2)154   **34.** 7)385   **35.** 4)168   **36.** 8)504

Division with Two-Digit Quotients and Remainders

Solve each problem.

Super Work!

1. $4\overline{)65}$ 2. $7\overline{)86}$ 3. $5\overline{)57}$ 4. $3\overline{)55}$

5. $2\overline{)35}$ 6. $2\overline{)87}$ 7. $3\overline{)74}$ 8. $6\overline{)81}$

9. $6\overline{)79}$ 10. $5\overline{)93}$ 11. $4\overline{)71}$ 12. $3\overline{)37}$

13. $3\overline{)95}$ 14. $3\overline{)64}$ 15. $7\overline{)79}$ 16. $3\overline{)68}$

17. $8\overline{)97}$ 18. $2\overline{)47}$ 19. $2\overline{)65}$ 20. $2\overline{)87}$

21. $6\overline{)75}$ 22. $8\overline{)97}$ 23. $5\overline{)72}$ 24. $7\overline{)79}$

25. $7\overline{)95}$ 26. $4\overline{)45}$ 27. $5\overline{)59}$ 28. $2\overline{)53}$

29. $2\overline{)83}$ 30. $3\overline{)74}$ 31. $4\overline{)53}$ 32. $3\overline{)47}$

33. $8\overline{)89}$ 34. $3\overline{)86}$ 35. $4\overline{)87}$ 36. $8\overline{)98}$

Name _____ Date _____

Division with Two-Digit Quotients and Remainders

Solve each problem. Show your work on another sheet of paper.
Write your answers here.

Jump to It!

1. 8)428   **2.** 5)338   **3.** 9)479   **4.** 4)358

5. 8)699   **6.** 9)245   **7.** 9)399   **8.** 4)314

9. 9)758   **10.** 8)389   **11.** 2)155   **12.** 6)175

13. 3)296   **14.** 3)209   **15.** 2)119   **16.** 5)439

17. 6)273   **18.** 4)345   **19.** 7)408   **20.** 6)392

21. 6)237   **22.** 8)597   **23.** 2)171   **24.** 4)231

25. 5)197   **26.** 6)507   **27.** 2)137   **28.** 7)549

29. 4)277   **30.** 3)173   **31.** 7)279   **32.** 5)291

33. 6)319   **34.** 5)238   **35.** 3)230   **36.** 2)173

Name _____   Date _____

Division with Two-Digit Quotients and Remainders

Solve each problem. Show your work on another sheet of paper. Write your answers here.

Division Will Take You Places!

1. $6\overline{)537}$ 2. $7\overline{)331}$ 3. $6\overline{)446}$ 4. $2\overline{)135}$

5. $8\overline{)210}$ 6. $8\overline{)756}$ 7. $9\overline{)291}$ 8. $5\overline{)374}$

9. $4\overline{)269}$ 10. $8\overline{)307}$ 11. $3\overline{)143}$ 12. $9\overline{)578}$

13. $2\overline{)157}$ 14. $9\overline{)659}$ 15. $2\overline{)179}$ 16. $8\overline{)532}$

17. $5\overline{)484}$ 18. $5\overline{)434}$ 19. $7\overline{)439}$ 20. $9\overline{)587}$

21. $4\overline{)155}$ 22. $6\overline{)562}$ 23. $7\overline{)489}$ 24. $7\overline{)736}$

25. $3\overline{)119}$ 26. $2\overline{)193}$ 27. $6\overline{)338}$ 28. $5\overline{)484}$

29. $8\overline{)532}$ 30. $8\overline{)649}$ 31. $8\overline{)757}$ 32. $3\overline{)224}$

33. $4\overline{)383}$ 34. $3\overline{)143}$ 35. $4\overline{)365}$ 36. $5\overline{)329}$

Division with Two-Digit Quotients and Remainders

Total Problems:	**36**
Problems Correct:	_____

Solve each problem. Show your work on another sheet of paper.
Write your answers here.

Take Off with Division!

1. 4)915

2. 6)652

3. 2)135

4. 9)867

5. 5)238

6. 9)245

7. 9)587

8. 3)224

9. 8)757

10. 6)446

11. 2)157

12. 2)137

13. 3)254

14. 4)383

15. 5)484

16. 8)953

17. 8)389

18. 9)291

19. 3)143

20. 3)119

21. 5)374

22. 7)331

23. 9)758

24. 3)209

25. 8)307

26. 4)269

27. 8)210

28. 6)338

29. 4)314

30. 7)439

31. 2)179

32. 9)659

33. 2)193

34. 6)537

35. 9)479

36. 6)392

Name _____ Date _____

Division with Two-Digit Quotients and Remainders

Solve each problem. Show your work on another sheet of paper.
Write your answers here.

5, 4, 3, 2, 1...Divide!

1. $4\overline{)315}$

2. $6\overline{)556}$

3. $2\overline{)135}$

4. $9\overline{)867}$

5. $5\overline{)238}$

6. $9\overline{)245}$

7. $9\overline{)587}$

8. $3\overline{)224}$

9. $8\overline{)757}$

10. $6\overline{)446}$

11. $2\overline{)157}$

12. $2\overline{)137}$

13. $2\overline{)179}$

14. $9\overline{)659}$

15. $2\overline{)193}$

16. $6\overline{)537}$

17. $9\overline{)479}$

18. $6\overline{)392}$

19. $3\overline{)254}$

20. $4\overline{)383}$

21. $5\overline{)484}$

22. $8\overline{)753}$

23. $8\overline{)389}$

24. $9\overline{)291}$

25. $3\overline{)143}$

26. $3\overline{)119}$

27. $5\overline{)374}$

28. $7\overline{)331}$

29. $9\overline{)758}$

30. $3\overline{)209}$

31. $8\overline{)307}$

32. $4\overline{)269}$

33. $8\overline{)210}$

34. $6\overline{)338}$

35. $4\overline{)314}$

36. $7\overline{)439}$

Division with Two- and Three-Digit Quotients

Total Problems: **36**
Problems Correct: _____

Solve each problem. Show your work on another sheet of paper.
Write your answers here.

Division Is a Blast!

1. 5)715

2. 3)942

3. 3)456

4. 7)854

5. 8)896

6. 3)312

7. 7)784

8. 9)999

9. 4)924

10. 8)896

11. 6)726

12. 7)777

13. 3)759

14. 4)856

15. 5)575

16. 3)945

17. 2)432

18. 6)654

19. 6)972

20. 2)548

21. 4)848

22. 2)746

23. 5)715

24. 4)420

25. 4)968

26. 4)932

27. 5)765

28. 5)585

29. 7)749

30. 9)189

31. 2)726

32. 2)952

33. 7)784

34. 6)786

35. 8)872

36. 7)217

Division with Three-Digit Quotients and Remainders

Solve each problem. Show your work on another sheet of paper.
Write your answers here.

Get a Head Start with Division!

1. $7\overline{)806}$ **2.** $4\overline{)759}$ **3.** $6\overline{)887}$ **4.** $7\overline{)858}$

5. $6\overline{)857}$ **6.** $6\overline{)676}$ **7.** $3\overline{)748}$ **8.** $3\overline{)836}$

9. $4\overline{)635}$ **10.** $8\overline{)899}$ **11.** $7\overline{)879}$ **12.** $8\overline{)978}$

13. $5\overline{)687}$ **14.** $6\overline{)987}$ **15.** $8\overline{)907}$ **16.** $4\overline{)595}$

17. $5\overline{)947}$ **18.** $2\overline{)337}$ **19.** $2\overline{)379}$ **20.** $6\overline{)739}$

21. $4\overline{)675}$ **22.** $2\overline{)537}$ **23.** $2\overline{)487}$ **24.** $5\overline{)684}$

25. $3\overline{)596}$ **26.** $5\overline{)994}$ **27.** $7\overline{)858}$ **28.** $6\overline{)689}$

29. $3\overline{)953}$ **30.** $3\overline{)647}$ **31.** $2\overline{)753}$ **32.** $5\overline{)734}$

33. $5\overline{)748}$ **34.** $5\overline{)893}$ **35.** $4\overline{)538}$ **36.** $4\overline{)629}$

Division with Two- and Three-Digit Quotients and Remainders

Solve each problem. Show your work on another sheet of paper.
Write your answers here.

Ready, Set, Divide!

1. $4\overline{)83}$ 2. $4\overline{)323}$ 3. $4\overline{)842}$ 4. $6\overline{)543}$

5. $5\overline{)404}$ 6. $4\overline{)283}$ 7. $5\overline{)526}$ 8. $4\overline{)842}$

9. $5\overline{)453}$ 10. $7\overline{)634}$ 11. $8\overline{)865}$ 12. $2\overline{)421}$

13. $8\overline{)87}$ 14. $3\overline{)623}$ 15. $6\overline{)364}$ 16. $3\overline{)631}$

17. $5\overline{)253}$ 18. $8\overline{)726}$ 19. $6\overline{)423}$ 20. $8\overline{)327}$

21. $4\overline{)483}$ 22. $9\overline{)938}$ 23. $4\overline{)414}$ 24. $5\overline{)517}$

25. $2\overline{)241}$ 26. $3\overline{)272}$ 27. $8\overline{)839}$ 28. $7\overline{)738}$

29. $7\overline{)423}$ 30. $9\overline{)98}$ 31. $7\overline{)738}$ 32. $2\overline{)615}$

33. $3\overline{)92}$ 34. $6\overline{)627}$ 35. $8\overline{)325}$ 36. $7\overline{)426}$

Name _____   Date _____

Division with Two- and Three-Digit Quotients and Remainders

Solve each problem. Show your work on another sheet of paper. Write your answers here.

Stir It Up with Division!

1. 3)623   2. 8)825   3. 9)98   4. 5)404

5. 2)461   6. 4)414   7. 5)529   8. 4)323

9. 2)615   10. 8)726   11. 6)364   12. 8)865

13. 4)283   14. 5)539   15. 2)841   16. 3)272

17. 4)823   18. 6)627   19. 2)421   20. 5)517

21. 7)426   22. 3)925   23. 6)827   24. 7)423

25. 7)738   26. 3)272   27. 4)842   28. 5)526

29. 5)453   30. 3)623   31. 6)423   32. 8)327

33. 3)961   34. 5)53   35. 7)738   36. 5)253

Division with Four-Digit Dividends

Solve each problem. Show your work on another sheet of paper.
Write your answers here.

Now You're Cooking!

1. $6\overline{)7{,}391}$

2. $3\overline{)2{,}874}$

3. $3\overline{)6{,}238}$

4. $8\overline{)4{,}376}$

5. $6\overline{)3{,}764}$

6. $9\overline{)2{,}819}$

7. $2\overline{)8{,}497}$

8. $6\overline{)8{,}149}$

9. $5\overline{)3{,}381}$

10. $4\overline{)2{,}988}$

11. $2\overline{)8{,}040}$

12. $3\overline{)3{,}788}$

13. $7\overline{)5{,}001}$

14. $2\overline{)6{,}841}$

15. $6\overline{)9{,}469}$

16. $5\overline{)5{,}328}$

17. $5\overline{)7{,}384}$

18. $4\overline{)5{,}978}$

19. $4\overline{)1{,}538}$

20. $2\overline{)4{,}811}$

21. $7\overline{)8{,}598}$

22. $4\overline{)8{,}572}$

23. $3\overline{)6{,}943}$

24. $6\overline{)6{,}432}$

25. $8\overline{)4{,}687}$

26. $5\overline{)5{,}237}$

27. $7\overline{)4{,}795}$

28. $2\overline{)3{,}486}$

29. $4\overline{)9{,}035}$

30. $7\overline{)4{,}001}$

Name _____ Date _____

Division with Two-Digit Divisors and Remainders

Solve each problem. Show your work on another sheet of paper.
Write your answers here.

Stretch Your Brain with Division!

1. $98\overline{)99}$ 2. $40\overline{)87}$ 3. $48\overline{)97}$ 4. $34\overline{)74}$

5. $21\overline{)87}$ 6. $19\overline{)28}$ 7. $19\overline{)88}$ 8. $37\overline{)86}$

9. $38\overline{)83}$ 10. $14\overline{)73}$ 11. $19\overline{)78}$ 12. $20\overline{)69}$

13. $24\overline{)82}$ 14. $25\overline{)61}$ 15. $22\overline{)90}$ 16. $18\overline{)61}$

17. $22\overline{)87}$ 18. $23\overline{)79}$ 19. $29\overline{)93}$ 20. $23\overline{)70}$

21. $28\overline{)96}$ 22. $14\overline{)85}$ 23. $18\overline{)93}$ 24. $17\overline{)59}$

25. $76\overline{)94}$ 26. $35\overline{)81}$ 27. $18\overline{)93}$ 28. $15\overline{)84}$

29. $21\overline{)77}$ 30. $84\overline{)85}$ 31. $42\overline{)93}$ 32. $12\overline{)75}$

33. $21\overline{)64}$ 34. $13\overline{)96}$ 35. $77\overline{)92}$ 36. $78\overline{)90}$

Name _____ Date _____

Division with Two-Digit Divisors and Remainders

Total Problems: **36**
Problems Correct: _____

Solve each problem. Show your work on another sheet of paper.
Write your answers here.

Math Is the Cat's Meow!

1. $22\overline{)419}$ 2. $18\overline{)822}$ 3. $82\overline{)833}$ 4. $26\overline{)375}$

5. $38\overline{)971}$ 6. $17\overline{)998}$ 7. $31\overline{)563}$ 8. $68\overline{)878}$

9. $32\overline{)847}$ 10. $35\overline{)819}$ 11. $67\overline{)973}$ 12. $24\overline{)527}$

13. $31\overline{)827}$ 14. $77\overline{)970}$ 15. $12\overline{)777}$ 16. $47\overline{)822}$

17. $88\overline{)995}$ 18. $42\overline{)710}$ 19. $58\overline{)902}$ 20. $94\overline{)977}$

21. $17\overline{)366}$ 22. $41\overline{)886}$ 23. $43\overline{)884}$ 24. $25\overline{)591}$

25. $36\overline{)915}$ 26. $57\overline{)787}$ 27. $84\overline{)927}$ 28. $91\overline{)952}$

29. $34\overline{)819}$ 30. $51\overline{)555}$ 31. $71\overline{)977}$ 32. $46\overline{)821}$

33. $53\overline{)948}$ 34. $75\overline{)888}$ 35. $19\overline{)777}$ 36. $27\overline{)845}$

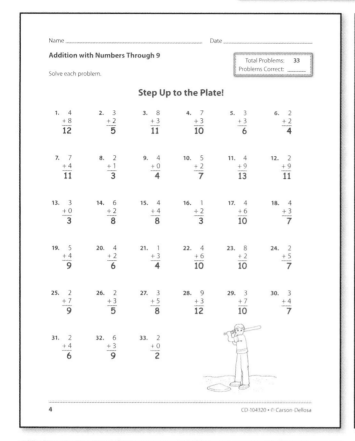

Name _____ Date _____

Addition with Numbers Through 9

Solve each problem.

Total Problems: **33**
Problems Correct: _____

Step Up to the Plate!

1. 4 + 8 **12**	2. 3 + 2 **5**	3. 8 + 3 **11**	4. 7 + 3 **10**	5. 3 + 3 **6**	6. 2 + 2 **4**
7. 7 + 4 **11**	8. 2 + 1 **3**	9. 4 + 0 **4**	10. 5 + 2 **7**	11. 4 + 9 **13**	12. 2 + 9 **11**
13. 3 + 0 **3**	14. 6 + 2 **8**	15. 4 + 4 **8**	16. 1 + 2 **3**	17. 4 + 6 **10**	18. 4 + 3 **7**
19. 5 + 4 **9**	20. 4 + 2 **6**	21. 1 + 3 **4**	22. 4 + 6 **10**	23. 8 + 2 **10**	24. 2 + 5 **7**
25. 2 + 7 **9**	26. 2 + 3 **5**	27. 3 + 5 **8**	28. 9 + 3 **12**	29. 3 + 7 **10**	30. 3 + 4 **7**
31. 2 + 4 **6**	32. 6 + 3 **9**	33. 2 + 0 **2**			

4   CD-104320 • © Carson-Dellosa

Name _____ Date _____

Addition with Numbers Through 9

Solve each problem.

Total Problems: **33**
Problems Correct: _____

Practice Makes Perfect!

1. 7 + 6 **13**	2. 7 + 7 **14**	3. 3 + 6 **9**	4. 4 + 3 **7**	5. 7 + 4 **11**	6. 5 + 4 **9**
7. 6 + 5 **11**	8. 9 + 8 **17**	9. 8 + 4 **12**	10. 6 + 2 **8**	11. 3 + 2 **5**	12. 3 + 9 **12**
13. 3 + 3 **6**	14. 9 + 5 **14**	15. 9 + 6 **15**	16. 2 + 7 **9**	17. 6 + 4 **10**	18. 5 + 8 **13**
19. 3 + 7 **10**	20. 6 + 8 **14**	21. 8 + 3 **11**	22. 5 + 4 **9**	23. 9 + 1 **10**	24. 9 + 8 **17**
25. 2 + 3 **5**	26. 3 + 5 **8**	27. 8 + 9 **17**	28. 4 + 3 **7**	29. 8 + 8 **16**	30. 3 + 3 **6**
31. 9 + 7 **16**	32. 8 + 7 **15**	33. 7 + 3 **10**			

CD-104320 • © Carson-Dellosa   5

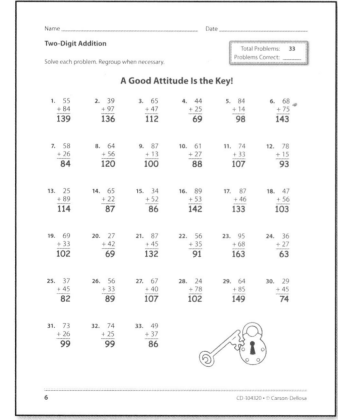

Name _____ Date _____

Two-Digit Addition

Solve each problem. Regroup when necessary.

Total Problems: **33**
Problems Correct: _____

A Good Attitude Is the Key!

1. 55 + 84 **139**	2. 39 + 97 **136**	3. 65 + 47 **112**	4. 44 + 25 **69**	5. 84 + 14 **98**	6. 68 + 75 **143**
7. 58 + 26 **84**	8. 64 + 56 **120**	9. 87 + 13 **100**	10. 61 + 27 **88**	11. 74 + 33 **107**	12. 78 + 15 **93**
13. 25 + 89 **114**	14. 65 + 22 **87**	15. 34 + 52 **86**	16. 89 + 53 **142**	17. 87 + 46 **133**	18. 47 + 56 **103**
19. 69 + 33 **102**	20. 27 + 42 **69**	21. 87 + 45 **132**	22. 56 + 35 **91**	23. 95 + 68 **163**	24. 36 + 27 **63**
25. 37 + 45 **82**	26. 56 + 33 **89**	27. 67 + 40 **107**	28. 24 + 78 **102**	29. 64 + 85 **149**	30. 29 + 45 **74**
31. 73 + 26 **99**	32. 74 + 25 **99**	33. 49 + 37 **86**			

6   CD-104320 • © Carson-Dellosa

Name _____ Date _____

Two-Digit Column Addition

Solve each problem. Regroup when necessary.

Total Problems: **22**
Problems Correct: _____

Unlock the Secrets of Addition!

1. 24 41 + 32 **97**	2. 91 28 + 13 **132**	3. 35 66 + 37 **138**	4. 22 61 + 84 **167**	5. 16 10 + 31 **57**	6. 45 32 + 48 **125**
7. 45 52 + 21 **118**	8. 28 39 + 21 **88**	9. 27 65 + 85 **177**	10. 74 26 + 39 **139**	11. 55 21 + 37 **113**	12. 33 30 + 36 **99**
13. 57 42 + 33 **132**	14. 38 46 + 23 **107**	15. 17 36 + 22 **75**	16. 85 36 + 74 **195**	17. 76 23 + 67 **166**	18. 56 21 + 32 **109**
19. 39 48 + 59 **146**	20. 45 23 + 54 **122**	21. 24 51 + 76 **151**	22. 25 45 + 56 **126**		

CD-104320 • © Carson-Dellosa   7

Page 8

Name _____ Date _____

Three-Digit Addition with Regrouping

Total Problems: 27
Problems Correct: _____

Solve each problem. Regroup when necessary.

Math Is a Gift!

1. 634 + 268 = **902**
2. 987 + 489 = **1,476**
3. 493 + 277 = **770**
4. 888 + 277 = **1,165**
5. 732 + 299 = **1,031**
6. 276 + 947 = **1,223**

7. 394 + 496 = **890**
8. 557 + 323 = **880**
9. 254 + 347 = **601**
10. 665 + 337 = **1,002**
11. 493 + 229 = **722**
12. 988 + 748 = **1,736**

13. 376 + 266 = **642**
14. 349 + 233 = **582**
15. 878 + 287 = **1,165**
16. 436 + 296 = **732**
17. 348 + 948 = **1,296**
18. 498 + 439 = **937**

19. 477 + 298 = **775**
20. 396 + 474 = **870**
21. 901 + 109 = **1,010**
22. 834 + 249 = **1,083**
23. 499 + 292 = **791**
24. 118 + 953 = **1,071**

25. 549 + 202 = **751**
26. 653 + 307 = **960**
27. 476 + 498 = **974**

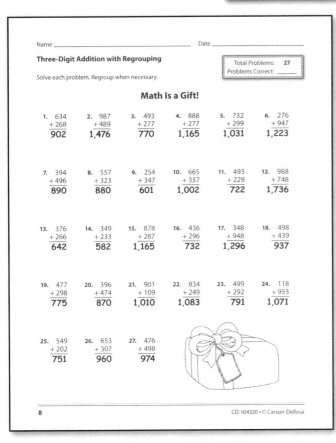

8   CD-104320 • © Carson-Dellosa

Page 9

Name _____ Date _____

Three-Digit Addition with Regrouping

Total Problems: 33
Problems Correct: _____

Solve each problem. Regroup when necessary.

Get Wrapped Up in Addition!

1. 566 + 467 = **1,033**
2. 979 + 354 = **1,333**
3. 945 + 379 = **1,324**
4. 888 + 276 = **1,164**
5. 871 + 739 = **1,610**
6. 478 + 655 = **1,133**

7. 675 + 597 = **1,272**
8. 456 + 327 = **783**
9. 254 + 347 = **601**
10. 349 + 493 = **842**
11. 765 + 428 = **1,193**
12. 834 + 666 = **1,500**

13. 238 + 348 = **586**
14. 349 + 233 = **582**
15. 434 + 948 = **1,382**
16. 869 + 572 = **1,441**
17. 458 + 749 = **1,207**
18. 638 + 422 = **1,060**

19. 539 + 468 = **1,007**
20. 396 + 578 = **974**
21. 955 + 134 = **1,089**
22. 367 + 984 = **1,351**
23. 588 + 294 = **882**
24. 493 + 327 = **820**

25. 669 + 291 = **960**
26. 455 + 347 = **802**
27. 646 + 668 = **1,314**
28. 877 + 353 = **1,230**
29. 123 + 238 = **361**
30. 348 + 489 = **837**

31. 239 + 593 = **832**
32. 159 + 485 = **644**
33. 648 + 437 = **1,085**

CD-104320 • © Carson-Dellosa   9

Page 10

Name _____ Date _____

Two-, Three-, and Four-Digit Column Addition with Regrouping

Total Problems: 22
Problems Correct: _____

Solve each problem. Regroup when necessary.

You're a Winner!

1. 3,878 + 4,981 + 8,165 = **17,024**
2. 9,651 + 3,321 + 2,283 = **15,255**
3. 3,981 + 2,357 + 4,652 = **10,990**
4. 76 + 59 + 53 = **188**
5. 34 + 67 + 24 = **125**
6. 776 + 453 + 719 = **1,948**

7. 5,349 + 3,274 + 7,184 = **15,807**
8. 676 + 734 + 651 = **2,061**
9. 7,028 + 4,354 + 5,684 = **17,066**
10. 6,048 + 3,278 + 5,328 = **14,654**
11. 4,348 + 3,451 + 2,734 = **10,533**
12. 343 + 608 + 789 = **1,740**

13. 4,340 + 5,433 + 3,238 = **13,011**
14. 356 + 674 + 380 = **1,410**
15. 54 + 39 + 73 = **166**
16. 634 + 198 + 518 = **1,350**
17. 67 + 98 + 74 = **239**
18. 5,367 + 3,190 + 1,499 = **10,056**

19. 47 + 34 + 99 = **180**
20. 321 + 436 + 548 = **1,305**
21. 2,783 + 2,546 + 6,748 = **12,077**
22. 9,418 + 8,009 + 7,245 = **24,672**

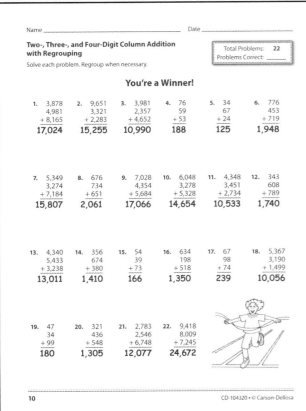

10   CD-104320 • © Carson-Dellosa

Page 11

Name _____ Date _____

Three- and Four-Digit Column Addition with Regrouping

Total Problems: 22
Problems Correct: _____

Solve each problem. Regroup when necessary.

Go for the Gold!

1. 378 + 943 + 549 = **1,870**
2. 6,382 + 7,452 + 6,789 = **20,623**
3. 435 + 526 + 268 = **1,229**
4. 526 + 452 + 498 = **1,476**
5. 528 + 754 + 294 = **1,576**
6. 652 + 751 + 439 = **1,842**

7. 3,658 + 2,814 + 3,856 = **10,328**
8. 457 + 989 + 276 = **1,722**
9. 7,458 + 4,349 + 5,962 = **17,769**
10. 6,356 + 5,093 + 3,637 = **15,086**
11. 8,236 + 5,548 + 5,327 = **19,111**
12. 5,256 + 8,248 + 4,241 = **17,745**

13. 6,898 + 5,433 + 2,154 = **14,485**
14. 8,459 + 4,908 + 4,356 = **17,723**
15. 525 + 653 + 896 = **2,074**
16. 5,265 + 2,278 + 8,365 = **15,908**
17. 2,147 + 3,255 + 2,256 = **7,658**
18. 654 + 452 + 138 = **1,244**

19. 7,092 + 5,405 + 6,124 = **18,621**
20. 5,768 + 6,937 + 7,034 = **19,739**
21. 4,265 + 5,124 + 6,489 = **15,878**
22. 8,214 + 7,716 + 6,389 = **22,319**

CD-104320 • © Carson-Dellosa   11

Worksheet (page 12)

Name _____ Date _____

Four-Digit Addition with Regrouping

Solve each problem. Regroup when necessary.

Total Problems: 33
Problems Correct: _____

Fly High with Math!

#		#		#		#		#		#	
1.	4,936 + 5,432 = **10,368**	2.	9,675 + 4,283 = **13,958**	3.	5,349 + 6,393 = **11,742**	4.	6,434 + 6,398 = **12,832**	5.	9,231 + 5,332 = **14,563**	6.	7,221 + 2,418 = **9,639**
7.	6,376 + 2,019 = **8,395**	8.	2,393 + 4,392 = **6,785**	9.	8,293 + 4,239 = **12,532**	10.	3,768 + 5,949 = **9,717**	11.	1,665 + 3,773 = **5,438**	12.	2,343 + 7,328 = **9,671**
13.	7,320 + 5,394 = **12,714**	14.	9,347 + 7,323 = **16,670**	15.	8,659 + 9,347 = **18,006**	16.	3,424 + 9,483 = **12,907**	17.	6,784 + 1,296 = **8,080**	18.	4,392 + 4,959 = **9,351**
19.	1,749 + 2,323 = **4,072**	20.	8,459 + 4,398 = **12,857**	21.	6,437 + 7,219 = **13,656**	22.	3,829 + 2,933 = **6,762**	23.	5,845 + 2,568 = **8,413**	24.	3,490 + 6,349 = **9,839**
25.	5,344 + 6,349 = **11,693**	26.	3,282 + 5,342 = **8,624**	27.	5,349 + 8,563 = **13,912**	28.	4,372 + 7,839 = **12,211**	29.	7,841 + 6,760 = **14,601**	30.	2,404 + 8,403 = **10,807**
31.	3,203 + 5,893 = **9,096**	32.	8,349 + 7,346 = **15,695**	33.	8,453 + 4,267 = **12,720**							

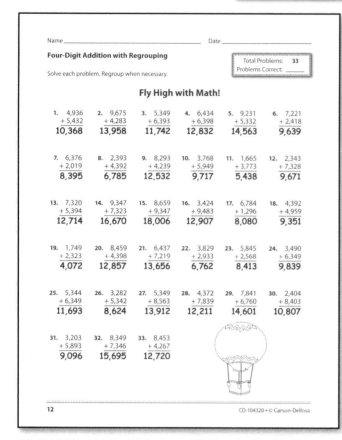

Worksheet (page 13)

Name _____ Date _____

Four-Digit Addition with Regrouping

Solve each problem. Regroup when necessary.

Total Problems: 33
Problems Correct: _____

Up, Up, Up and Away with Addition!

#		#		#		#		#		#	
1.	3,878 + 8,456 = **12,334**	2.	9,675 + 4,283 = **13,958**	3.	3,534 + 4,652 = **8,186**	4.	8,900 + 3,957 = **12,857**	5.	9,231 + 5,332 = **14,563**	6.	8,569 + 2,546 = **11,115**
7.	6,376 + 2,019 = **8,395**	8.	5,349 + 7,345 = **12,694**	9.	4,324 + 5,769 = **10,093**	10.	6,909 + 3,212 = **10,121**	11.	7,458 + 5,494 = **12,952**	12.	2,343 + 7,328 = **9,671**
13.	4,348 + 2,734 = **7,082**	14.	5,343 + 8,223 = **13,566**	15.	8,999 + 3,856 = **12,855**	16.	4,340 + 3,264 = **7,604**	17.	8,456 + 4,380 = **12,836**	18.	4,392 + 4,959 = **9,351**
19.	3,234 + 2,923 = **6,157**	20.	4,348 + 9,574 = **13,922**	21.	7,090 + 5,845 = **12,935**	22.	5,345 + 1,433 = **6,778**	23.	3,287 + 5,122 = **8,409**	24.	3,490 + 6,349 = **9,839**
25.	4,346 + 6,333 = **10,679**	26.	9,895 + 7,459 = **17,354**	27.	7,989 + 5,915 = **13,904**	28.	3,259 + 6,323 = **9,582**	29.	6,381 + 6,743 = **13,124**	30.	2,404 + 8,654 = **11,058**
31.	4,646 + 3,984 = **8,630**	32.	5,913 + 2,264 = **8,177**	33.	8,964 + 1,651 = **10,615**							

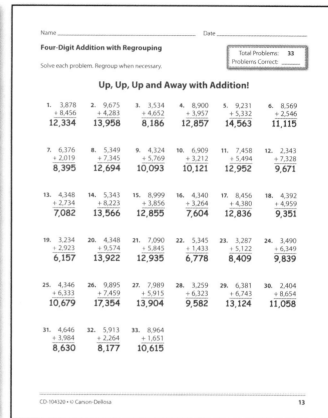

Worksheet (page 14)

Name _____ Date _____

Addition of Decimals

Solve each problem. Regroup when necessary.

Total Problems: 33
Problems Correct: _____

Keep Your Focus!

#		#		#		#		#		#	
1.	6.34 + 2.68 = **9.02**	2.	9.87 + 4.89 = **14.76**	3.	4.93 + 2.77 = **7.70**	4.	8.88 + 2.76 = **11.64**	5.	7.32 + 2.99 = **10.31**	6.	2.76 + 9.47 = **12.23**
7.	3.94 + 4.96 = **8.90**	8.	5.57 + 3.23 = **8.80**	9.	2.54 + 3.47 = **6.01**	10.	6.65 + 3.37 = **10.02**	11.	4.93 + 2.29 = **7.22**	12.	9.88 + 7.48 = **17.36**
13.	3.76 + 2.66 = **6.42**	14.	3.49 + 2.33 = **5.82**	15.	8.78 + 2.87 = **11.65**	16.	4.36 + 2.96 = **7.32**	17.	3.48 + 9.48 = **12.96**	18.	4.98 + 4.39 = **9.37**
19.	4.77 + 2.98 = **7.75**	20.	3.96 + 4.74 = **8.70**	21.	9.01 + 1.09 = **10.10**	22.	8.34 + 2.49 = **10.83**	23.	4.99 + 2.92 = **7.91**	24.	1.18 + 9.53 = **10.71**
25.	5.49 + 2.02 = **7.51**	26.	6.53 + 3.07 = **9.60**	27.	4.76 + 4.98 = **9.74**	28.	9.45 + 3.68 = **13.13**	29.	1.13 + 2.98 = **4.11**	30.	3.93 + 2.98 = **6.91**
31.	2.36 + 5.87 = **8.23**	32.	2.57 + 5.86 = **8.43**	33.	5.47 + 2.49 = **7.96**							

Worksheet (page 15)

Name _____ Date _____

Addition of Decimals

Solve each problem. Regroup when necessary.

Total Problems: 33
Problems Correct: _____

Zooming Through Addition!

#		#		#		#		#		#	
1.	5.66 + 4.67 = **10.33**	2.	9.79 + 3.54 = **13.33**	3.	9.45 + 3.79 = **13.24**	4.	8.88 + 2.76 = **11.64**	5.	8.70 + 7.39 = **16.09**	6.	4.78 + 6.55 = **11.33**
7.	6.75 + 5.97 = **12.72**	8.	4.56 + 3.27 = **7.83**	9.	2.54 + 3.47 = **6.01**	10.	3.49 + 4.93 = **8.42**	11.	7.65 + 4.28 = **11.93**	12.	8.34 + 6.65 = **14.99**
13.	2.38 + 3.48 = **5.86**	14.	3.49 + 2.33 = **5.82**	15.	4.34 + 9.48 = **13.82**	16.	8.69 + 5.72 = **14.41**	17.	4.58 + 7.49 = **12.07**	18.	6.38 + 4.22 = **10.60**
19.	5.39 + 4.68 = **10.07**	20.	3.96 + 5.78 = **9.74**	21.	9.55 + 1.34 = **10.89**	22.	3.67 + 9.84 = **13.51**	23.	5.88 + 2.94 = **8.82**	24.	4.93 + 3.27 = **8.20**
25.	6.46 + 2.91 = **9.37**	26.	4.55 + 3.47 = **8.02**	27.	6.46 + 6.68 = **13.14**	28.	8.77 + 3.52 = **12.29**	29.	1.23 + 2.38 = **3.61**	30.	3.48 + 4.89 = **8.37**
31.	2.39 + 5.93 = **8.32**	32.	1.59 + 4.85 = **6.44**	33.	6.48 + 4.37 = **10.85**							

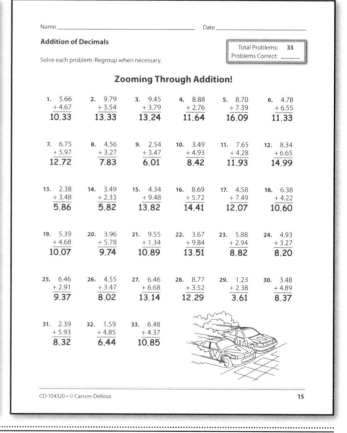

Page 16 — Addition of Decimals

Name _____ Date _____

Addition of Decimals

Solve each problem. Regroup when necessary.

Total Problems: 33
Problems Correct: _____

You're Doing It!

1. $49.36 + 54.32 = 103.68$
2. $96.75 + 42.83 = 139.58$
3. $53.49 + 63.93 = 117.42$
4. $64.34 + 63.98 = 128.32$
5. $92.31 + 53.32 = 145.63$
6. $72.21 + 24.18 = 96.39$

7. $63.76 + 20.19 = 83.95$
8. $23.93 + 43.68 = 67.61$
9. $82.93 + 42.18 = 125.11$
10. $37.68 + 59.37 = 97.05$
11. $16.65 + 37.73 = 54.38$
12. $23.43 + 73.28 = 96.71$

13. $73.20 + 53.94 = 127.14$
14. $93.47 + 73.23 = 166.70$
15. $86.59 + 93.47 = 180.06$
16. $34.24 + 94.83 = 129.07$
17. $67.84 + 12.96 = 80.80$
18. $43.92 + 49.28 = 93.20$

19. $17.49 + 23.23 = 40.72$
20. $84.77 + 43.12 = 127.89$
21. $64.37 + 72.19 = 136.56$
22. $38.29 + 29.33 = 67.62$
23. $58.45 + 25.68 = 84.13$
24. $34.90 + 63.49 = 98.39$

25. $53.44 + 67.90 = 121.34$
26. $32.02 + 53.78 = 85.80$
27. $53.49 + 85.63 = 139.12$
28. $43.72 + 78.39 = 122.11$
29. $78.41 + 67.60 = 146.01$
30. $24.04 + 84.03 = 108.07$

31. $32.03 + 53.68 = 85.71$
32. $84.53 + 42.67 = 127.20$
33. $83.18 + 73.46 = 156.64$

16 — CD-104320 • © Carson-Dellosa

Page 17 — Addition of Decimals

Name _____ Date _____

Addition of Decimals

Solve each problem. Regroup when necessary.

Total Problems: 33
Problems Correct: _____

You're a Success!

1. $38.78 + 84.56 = 123.34$
2. $96.75 + 42.83 = 139.58$
3. $32.34 + 46.52 = 78.86$
4. $89.00 + 39.57 = 128.57$
5. $92.31 + 53.32 = 145.63$
6. $85.69 + 25.46 = 111.15$

7. $63.76 + 20.19 = 83.95$
8. $53.49 + 73.45 = 126.94$
9. $43.24 + 57.69 = 100.93$
10. $69.09 + 32.12 = 101.21$
11. $74.58 + 54.94 = 129.52$
12. $23.43 + 73.28 = 96.71$

13. $43.48 + 27.34 = 70.82$
14. $53.43 + 82.23 = 135.66$
15. $89.99 + 38.56 = 128.55$
16. $43.40 + 32.34 = 75.74$
17. $84.56 + 43.80 = 128.36$
18. $43.92 + 49.59 = 93.51$

19. $32.34 + 23.23 = 55.57$
20. $43.48 + 95.74 = 139.22$
21. $70.90 + 58.45 = 129.35$
22. $53.45 + 14.35 = 67.80$
23. $32.87 + 51.22 = 84.09$
24. $34.90 + 63.49 = 98.39$

25. $43.46 + 63.33 = 106.79$
26. $98.95 + 74.59 = 173.54$
27. $79.89 + 59.15 = 139.04$
28. $32.59 + 63.23 = 95.82$
29. $63.81 + 37.43 = 101.24$
30. $24.04 + 84.03 = 108.07$

31. $43.84 + 32.51 = 76.35$
32. $52.38 + 28.41 = 80.79$
33. $83.45 + 14.89 = 98.34$

CD-104320 • © Carson-Dellosa — 17

Page 18 — Addition of Fractions

Name _____ Date _____

Addition of Fractions

Solve each problem. Write the answer in its simplest form.

Total Problems: 15
Problems Correct: _____

Let's Go for a Ride!

1. $\frac{1}{3} + \frac{2}{3} = 1$
2. $\frac{2}{9} + \frac{5}{9} = \frac{7}{9}$
3. $\frac{1}{6} + \frac{1}{6} = \frac{1}{3}$

4. $\frac{3}{6} + \frac{1}{6} = \frac{2}{3}$
5. $\frac{2}{4} + \frac{2}{4} = 1$
6. $\frac{1}{2} + \frac{1}{2} = 1$

7. $\frac{5}{8} + \frac{3}{8} = 1$
8. $\frac{5}{5} + \frac{2}{5} = 1\frac{2}{5}$
9. $\frac{2}{10} + \frac{4}{10} = \frac{3}{5}$

10. $\frac{1}{4} + \frac{3}{4} = 1$
11. $\frac{3}{5} + \frac{2}{5} = 1$
12. $\frac{3}{7} + \frac{2}{7} = \frac{5}{7}$

13. $\frac{3}{4} + \frac{1}{4} = 1$
14. $\frac{1}{7} + \frac{1}{7} = \frac{2}{7}$
15. $\frac{1}{6} + \frac{4}{6} = \frac{5}{6}$

18 — CD-104320 • © Carson-Dellosa

Page 19 — Addition of Fractions

Name _____ Date _____

Addition of Fractions

Solve each problem. Write the answer in its simplest form.

Total Problems: 20
Problems Correct: _____

Have Fun with Fractions!

1. $\frac{2}{7} + \frac{3}{7} = \frac{5}{7}$
2. $\frac{6}{8} + \frac{1}{8} = \frac{7}{8}$
3. $\frac{7}{10} + \frac{9}{10} = 1\frac{3}{5}$
4. $\frac{3}{7} + \frac{1}{7} = \frac{4}{7}$
5. $\frac{1}{5} + \frac{3}{5} = \frac{4}{5}$

6. $\frac{3}{5} + \frac{3}{5} = 1\frac{1}{5}$
7. $\frac{1}{4} + \frac{2}{4} = \frac{3}{4}$
8. $\frac{1}{5} + \frac{3}{5} = \frac{4}{5}$
9. $\frac{4}{8} + \frac{2}{8} = \frac{3}{4}$
10. $\frac{6}{7} + \frac{5}{7} = 1\frac{4}{7}$

11. $\frac{1}{8} + \frac{5}{8} = \frac{3}{4}$
12. $\frac{2}{8} + \frac{4}{8} = \frac{3}{4}$
13. $\frac{2}{10} + \frac{4}{10} = \frac{3}{5}$
14. $\frac{3}{4} + \frac{2}{4} = 1\frac{1}{4}$
15. $\frac{2}{3} + \frac{1}{3} = 1$

16. $\frac{4}{9} + \frac{3}{9} = \frac{7}{9}$
17. $\frac{2}{6} + \frac{1}{6} = \frac{1}{2}$
18. $\frac{5}{12} + \frac{5}{12} = \frac{5}{6}$
19. $\frac{1}{6} + \frac{3}{6} = \frac{2}{3}$
20. $\frac{2}{9} + \frac{1}{9} = \frac{1}{3}$

CD-104320 • © Carson-Dellosa — 19

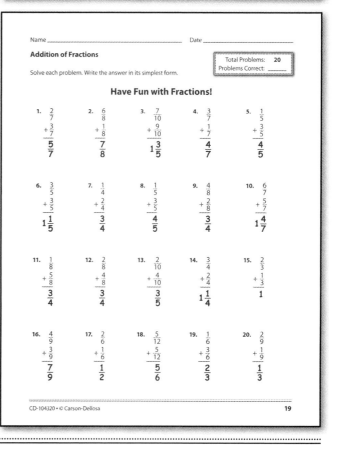

Subtraction with Numbers Through 12

Name _____ Date _____

Total Problems: **33**
Problems Correct: _____

Solve each problem.

Take Subtraction for a Spin!

1. 4 − 0 = **4**	2. 12 − 4 = **8**	3. 4 − 2 = **2**	4. 7 − 3 = **4**	5. 2 − 1 = **1**	6. 11 − 4 = **7**
7. 9 − 2 = **7**	8. 7 − 4 = **3**	9. 3 − 3 = **0**	10. 11 − 3 = **8**	11. 5 − 3 = **2**	12. 6 − 2 = **4**
13. 6 − 3 = **3**	14. 10 − 2 = **8**	15. 3 − 2 = **1**	16. 11 − 3 = **8**	17. 5 − 2 = **3**	18. 4 − 1 = **3**
19. 12 − 3 = **9**	20. 7 − 2 = **5**	21. 6 − 4 = **2**	22. 8 − 4 = **4**	23. 2 − 0 = **2**	24. 10 − 3 = **7**
25. 8 − 2 = **6**	26. 3 − 1 = **2**	27. 8 − 1 = **7**	28. 10 − 3 = **7**	29. 9 − 3 = **6**	30. 9 − 4 = **5**
31. 8 − 4 = **4**	32. 4 − 3 = **1**	33. 10 − 7 = **3**			

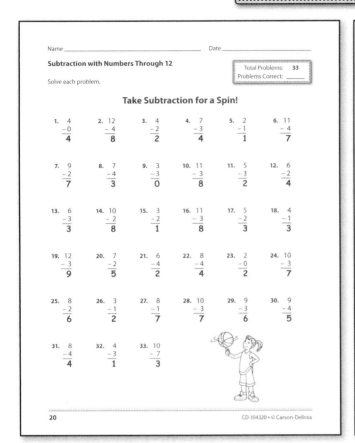

CD-104320 • © Carson-Dellosa

Subtraction with Numbers Through 18

Name _____ Date _____

Total Problems: **33**
Problems Correct: _____

Solve each problem.

You Can Handle It!

1. 15 − 8 = **7**	2. 11 − 6 = **5**	3. 14 − 7 = **7**	4. 10 − 6 = **4**	5. 8 − 0 = **8**	6. 12 − 7 = **5**
7. 12 − 5 = **7**	8. 14 − 8 = **6**	9. 10 − 7 = **3**	10. 8 − 6 = **2**	11. 13 − 8 = **5**	12. 9 − 6 = **3**
13. 6 − 0 = **6**	14. 16 − 7 = **9**	15. 7 − 0 = **7**	16. 7 − 5 = **2**	17. 15 − 6 = **9**	18. 10 − 8 = **2**
19. 16 − 6 = **10**	20. 8 − 1 = **7**	21. 12 − 8 = **4**	22. 18 − 8 = **10**	23. 8 − 8 = **0**	24. 9 − 7 = **2**
25. 7 − 1 = **6**	26. 13 − 6 = **7**	27. 6 − 1 = **5**	28. 14 − 6 = **8**	29. 14 − 7 = **7**	30. 7 − 6 = **1**
31. 9 − 8 = **1**	32. 10 − 7 = **3**	33. 8 − 3 = **5**			

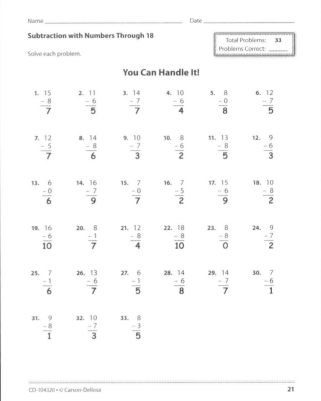

CD-104320 • © Carson-Dellosa

Subtraction with Numbers Through 19

Name _____ Date _____

Total Problems: **33**
Problems Correct: _____

Solve each problem.

Take Your Time!

1. 18 − 9 = **9**	2. 12 − 8 = **4**	3. 15 − 8 = **7**	4. 13 − 9 = **4**	5. 17 − 9 = **8**	6. 17 − 8 = **9**
7. 16 − 9 = **7**	8. 9 − 9 = **0**	9. 7 − 7 = **0**	10. 13 − 7 = **6**	11. 19 − 8 = **11**	12. 14 − 7 = **7**
13. 11 − 7 = **4**	14. 8 − 7 = **1**	15. 14 − 8 = **6**	16. 13 − 8 = **5**	17. 11 − 9 = **2**	18. 15 − 7 = **8**
19. 16 − 8 = **8**	20. 10 − 8 = **2**	21. 9 − 1 = **8**	22. 12 − 9 = **3**	23. 10 − 7 = **3**	24. 16 − 8 = **8**
25. 11 − 8 = **3**	26. 12 − 9 = **3**	27. 12 − 7 = **5**	28. 9 − 7 = **2**	29. 17 − 7 = **10**	30. 17 − 9 = **8**
31. 14 − 9 = **5**	32. 16 − 9 = **7**	33. 14 − 9 = **5**			

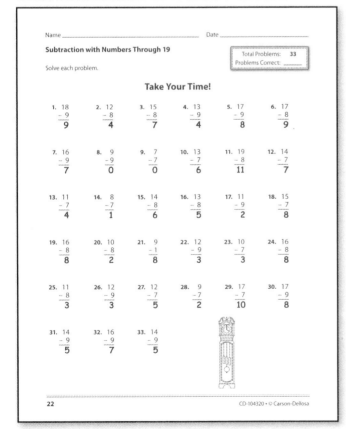

CD-104320 • © Carson-Dellosa

Subtraction with Numbers Through 19

Name _____ Date _____

Total Problems: **33**
Problems Correct: _____

Solve each problem.

Time to Subtract!

1. 4 − 3 = **1**	2. 7 − 3 = **4**	3. 13 − 6 = **7**	4. 5 − 3 = **2**	5. 19 − 4 = **15**	6. 15 − 7 = **8**
7. 17 − 8 = **9**	8. 9 − 2 = **7**	9. 15 − 8 = **7**	10. 11 − 6 = **5**	11. 16 − 9 = **7**	12. 8 − 1 = **7**
13. 8 − 5 = **3**	14. 9 − 4 = **5**	15. 6 − 2 = **4**	16. 18 − 7 = **11**	17. 7 − 2 = **5**	18. 12 − 8 = **4**
19. 12 − 7 = **5**	20. 9 − 6 = **3**	21. 9 − 1 = **8**	22. 10 − 5 = **5**	23. 14 − 9 = **5**	24. 8 − 4 = **4**
25. 13 − 9 = **4**	26. 6 − 4 = **2**	27. 11 − 5 = **6**	28. 14 − 8 = **6**	29. 15 − 6 = **9**	30. 19 − 9 = **10**
31. 16 − 7 = **9**	32. 14 − 5 = **9**	33. 6 − 1 = **5**			

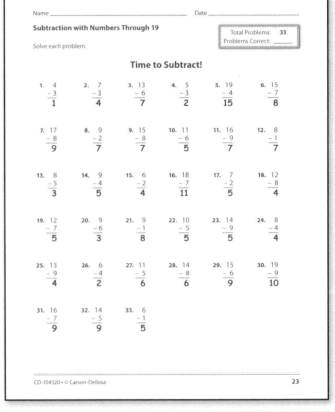

CD-104320 • © Carson-Dellosa

Two-Digit Subtraction

Name _____ Date _____

Solve each problem.

Total Problems: **33**
Problems Correct: _____

Give Subtraction a Whirl!

1. 82
   − 31
   51

2. 88
   − 32
   56

3. 86
   − 51
   35

4. 67
   − 42
   25

5. 75
   − 25
   50

6. 94
   − 60
   34

7. 98
   − 77
   21

8. 64
   − 31
   33

9. 37
   − 22
   15

10. 48
   − 24
   24

11. 56
   − 22
   34

12. 28
   − 15
   13

13. 75
   − 42
   33

14. 88
   − 66
   22

15. 87
   − 33
   54

16. 99
   − 65
   34

17. 78
   − 41
   37

18. 61
   − 30
   31

19. 65
   − 32
   33

20. 93
   − 52
   41

21. 88
   − 35
   53

22. 85
   − 73
   12

23. 95
   − 62
   33

24. 74
   − 42
   32

25. 36
   − 15
   21

26. 75
   − 53
   22

27. 76
   − 51
   25

28. 73
   − 21
   52

29. 39
   − 12
   27

30. 58
   − 33
   25

31. 43
   − 31
   12

32. 67
   − 12
   55

33. 85
   − 31
   54

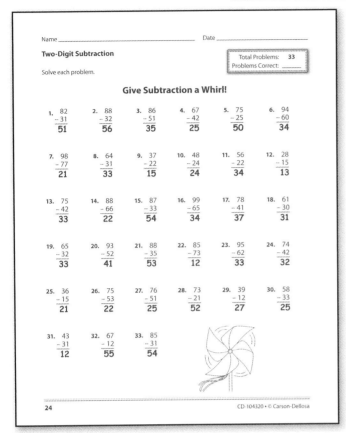

24   CD-104320 • © Carson-Dellosa

Two-Digit Subtraction with Regrouping

Name _____ Date _____

Solve each problem. Regroup when necessary.

Total Problems: **33**
Problems Correct: _____

Subtraction Is a Breeze!

1. 86
   − 38
   48

2. 73
   − 45
   28

3. 53
   − 37
   16

4. 48
   − 29
   19

5. 76
   − 68
   8

6. 64
   − 48
   16

7. 94
   − 58
   36

8. 42
   − 27
   15

9. 81
   − 53
   28

10. 66
   − 38
   28

11. 78
   − 59
   19

12. 72
   − 47
   25

13. 66
   − 38
   28

14. 97
   − 58
   39

15. 67
   − 18
   49

16. 66
   − 49
   17

17. 57
   − 29
   28

18. 36
   − 19
   17

19. 55
   − 49
   6

20. 55
   − 26
   29

21. 78
   − 49
   29

22. 91
   − 73
   18

23. 90
   − 33
   57

24. 86
   − 27
   59

25. 31
   − 23
   8

26. 46
   − 29
   17

27. 66
   − 47
   19

28. 74
   − 35
   39

29. 28
   − 19
   9

30. 63
   − 45
   18

31. 76
   − 49
   27

32. 70
   − 27
   43

33. 56
   − 39
   17

CD-104320 • © Carson-Dellosa   25

Two- and Three-Digit Subtraction with Regrouping

Name _____ Date _____

Solve each problem. Regroup when necessary.

Total Problems: **33**
Problems Correct: _____

Moo-ving Right Along!

1. 95
   − 66
   29

2. 812
   − 726
   86

3. 434
   − 356
   78

4. 769
   − 438
   331

5. 879
   − 389
   490

6. 49
   − 24
   25

7. 53
   − 27
   26

8. 82
   − 38
   44

9. 87
   − 78
   9

10. 726
   − 417
   309

11. 75
   − 58
   17

12. 87
   − 39
   48

13. 93
   − 46
   47

14. 78
   − 39
   39

15. 612
   − 538
   74

16. 800
   − 524
   276

17. 539
   − 366
   173

18. 576
   − 379
   197

19. 658
   − 377
   281

20. 632
   − 167
   465

21. 936
   − 687
   249

22. 841
   − 385
   456

23. 695
   − 289
   406

24. 625
   − 378
   247

25. 768
   − 579
   189

26. 798
   − 599
   199

27. 473
   − 128
   345

28. 635
   − 574
   61

29. 484
   − 299
   185

30. 832
   − 597
   235

31. 837
   − 376
   461

32. 536
   − 359
   177

33. 938
   − 377
   561

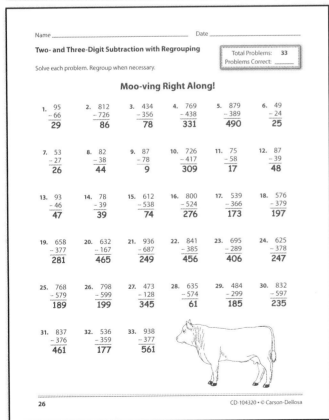

26   CD-104320 • © Carson-Dellosa

Three-Digit Subtraction with Regrouping

Name _____ Date _____

Solve each problem. Regroup when necessary.

Total Problems: **33**
Problems Correct: _____

Don't Have a Cow!

1. 736
   − 397
   339

2. 890
   − 249
   641

3. 768
   − 479
   289

4. 385
   − 269
   116

5. 747
   − 458
   289

6. 837
   − 209
   628

7. 476
   − 267
   209

8. 689
   − 478
   211

9. 677
   − 288
   389

10. 376
   − 187
   189

11. 521
   − 294
   227

12. 387
   − 329
   58

13. 301
   − 242
   59

14. 541
   − 377
   164

15. 471
   − 382
   89

16. 727
   − 419
   308

17. 848
   − 399
   449

18. 847
   − 358
   489

19. 502
   − 321
   181

20. 704
   − 597
   107

21. 846
   − 457
   389

22. 603
   − 277
   326

23. 405
   − 228
   177

24. 235
   − 128
   107

25. 703
   − 478
   225

26. 787
   − 548
   239

27. 584
   − 295
   289

28. 600
   − 367
   233

29. 400
   − 373
   27

30. 548
   − 369
   179

31. 834
   − 657
   177

32. 748
   − 259
   489

33. 748
   − 459
   289

CD-104320 • © Carson-Dellosa   27

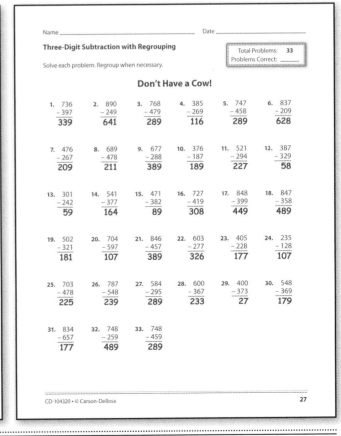

Three-Digit Subtraction with Regrouping

Name _____ Date _____

Total Problems:	33
Problems Correct:	_____

Solve each problem. Regroup when necessary.

Relax with Subtraction!

1. 784 − 591 = **193**
2. 547 − 265 = **282**
3. 622 − 323 = **299**
4. 825 − 638 = **187**
5. 923 − 568 = **355**
6. 950 − 580 = **370**

7. 663 − 271 = **392**
8. 967 − 794 = **173**
9. 982 − 398 = **584**
10. 293 − 187 = **106**
11. 732 − 467 = **265**
12. 824 − 548 = **276**

13. 845 − 566 = **279**
14. 429 − 188 = **241**
15. 659 − 478 = **181**
16. 725 − 469 = **256**
17. 827 − 577 = **250**
18. 536 − 459 = **78**

19. 527 − 265 = **262**
20. 574 − 293 = **281**
21. 557 − 278 = **279**
22. 423 − 155 = **268**
23. 766 − 577 = **189**
24. 536 − 258 = **278**

25. 677 − 289 = **388**
26. 857 − 675 = **182**
27. 783 − 399 = **384**
28. 748 − 353 = **395**
29. 831 − 357 = **474**
30. 521 − 245 = **276**

31. 940 − 565 = **375**
32. 438 − 254 = **184**
33. 487 − 378 = **109**

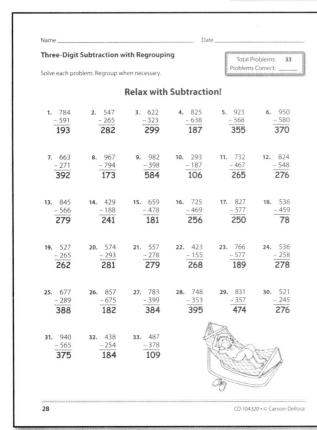

28 CD-104320 • © Carson-Dellosa

Three- and Four-Digit Subtraction with Regrouping

Name _____ Date _____

Total Problems:	27
Problems Correct:	_____

Solve each problem. Regroup when necessary.

Take It Easy!

1. 653 − 277 = **376**
2. 8,564 − 3,956 = **4,608**
3. 4,856 − 2,789 = **2,067**
4. 3,111 − 1,278 = **1,833**
5. 527 − 386 = **141**
6. 3,956 − 2,597 = **1,359**

7. 7,775 − 4,959 = **2,816**
8. 3,834 − 3,675 = **159**
9. 845 − 608 = **237**
10. 8,945 − 4,867 = **4,078**
11. 4,831 − 1,945 = **2,886**
12. 8,352 − 2,777 = **5,575**

13. 263 − 157 = **106**
14. 751 − 397 = **354**
15. 9,276 − 5,983 = **3,293**
16. 5,650 − 4,584 = **1,066**
17. 6,120 − 3,212 = **2,908**
18. 414 − 347 = **67**

19. 629 − 563 = **66**
20. 9,634 − 7,985 = **1,649**
21. 3,481 − 2,349 = **1,132**
22. 8,543 − 4,199 = **4,344**
23. 437 − 167 = **270**
24. 438 − 289 = **149**

25. 4,483 − 2,659 = **1,824**
26. 7,433 − 1,389 = **6,044**
27. 4,392 − 2,899 = **1,493**

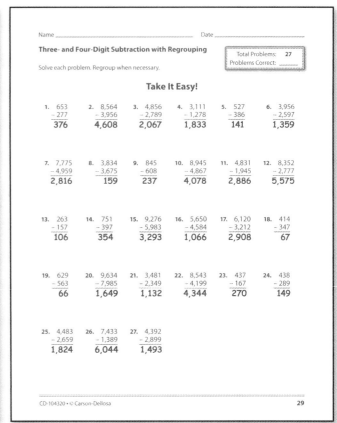

CD-104320 • © Carson-Dellosa 29

Four-Digit Subtraction with Regrouping

Name _____ Date _____

Total Problems:	27
Problems Correct:	_____

Solve each problem. Regroup when necessary.

Shoot for the Moon!

1. 9,534 − 2,389 = **7,145**
2. 5,464 − 2,756 = **2,708**
3. 3,526 − 1,653 = **1,873**
4. 3,354 − 2,328 = **1,026**
5. 5,247 − 3,836 = **1,411**
6. 8,456 − 3,462 = **4,994**

7. 4,755 − 3,875 = **880**
8. 7,243 − 2,376 = **4,867**
9. 6,845 − 4,764 = **2,081**
10. 5,935 − 3,837 = **2,098**
11. 4,376 − 2,438 = **1,938**
12. 9,122 − 4,547 = **4,575**

13. 2,643 − 1,439 = **1,204**
14. 3,765 − 3,498 = **267**
15. 7,236 − 2,276 = **4,960**
16. 7,340 − 5,364 = **1,976**
17. 6,849 − 4,114 = **2,735**
18. 7,414 − 2,838 = **4,576**

19. 6,249 − 5,633 = **616**
20. 8,344 − 4,754 = **3,590**
21. 8,363 − 6,476 = **1,887**
22. 7,221 − 5,347 = **1,874**
23. 4,343 − 3,278 = **1,065**
24. 3,567 − 2,853 = **714**

25. 5,277 − 1,654 = **3,623**
26. 9,644 − 5,842 = **3,802**
27. 6,694 − 4,851 = **1,843**

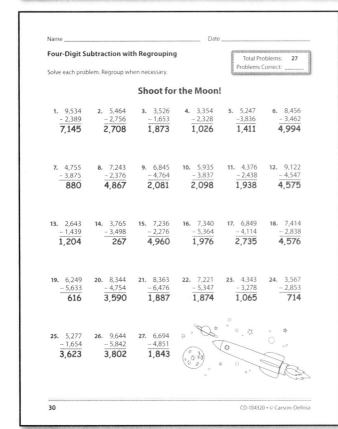

30 CD-104320 • © Carson-Dellosa

Four-Digit Subtraction

Name _____ Date _____

Total Problems:	27
Problems Correct:	_____

Solve each problem. Regroup when necessary.

You're a Star!

1. 7,687 − 2,438 = **5,249**
2. 3,465 − 1,854 = **1,611**
3. 6,895 − 2,957 = **3,938**
4. 4,568 − 3,489 = **1,079**
5. 7,264 − 6,966 = **298**
6. 8,346 − 6,478 = **1,868**

7. 6,894 − 2,785 = **4,109**
8. 7,945 − 3,329 = **4,616**
9. 2,348 − 1,365 = **983**
10. 8,232 − 3,984 = **4,248**
11. 6,189 − 2,312 = **3,877**
12. 8,909 − 7,498 = **1,411**

13. 4,879 − 2,782 = **2,097**
14. 7,493 − 4,691 = **2,802**
15. 6,349 − 2,542 = **3,807**
16. 4,393 − 2,765 = **1,628**
17. 9,347 − 3,659 = **5,688**
18. 8,785 − 4,934 = **3,851**

19. 7,946 − 7,745 = **201**
20. 8,238 − 7,459 = **779**
21. 4,319 − 2,880 = **1,439**
22. 3,769 − 2,424 = **1,345**
23. 4,111 − 2,648 = **1,463**
24. 4,846 − 2,845 = **2,001**

25. 8,945 − 5,289 = **3,656**
26. 4,349 − 2,375 = **1,974**
27. 3,020 − 2,303 = **717**

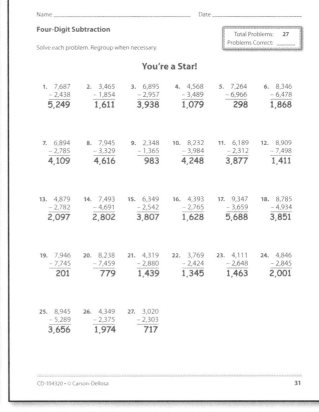

CD-104320 • © Carson-Dellosa 31

Worksheet 1 (page 32)

Name _____ Date _____

Five-Digit Subtraction

Total Problems: 27
Problems Correct: _____

Solve each problem. Regroup when necessary.

Hang in There!

#		#		#		#		#		#	
1.	34,347 − 23,564 = **10,783**	2.	54,347 − 35,756 = **18,591**	3.	53,768 − 44,768 = **9,000**	4.	68,498 − 56,856 = **11,642**	5.	59,547 − 48,945 = **10,602**	6.	78,345 − 43,274 = **35,071**
7.	86,423 − 83,575 = **2,848**	8.	65,567 − 56,980 = **8,587**	9.	72,894 − 67,989 = **4,905**	10.	78,960 − 56,809 = **22,151**	11.	76,378 − 35,789 = **40,589**	12.	43,698 − 25,435 = **18,263**
13.	76,453 − 47,456 = **28,997**	14.	78,498 − 56,843 = **21,655**	15.	56,896 − 52,908 = **3,988**	16.	43,645 − 34,883 = **8,762**	17.	64,348 − 21,212 = **43,136**	18.	98,456 − 89,564 = **8,892**
19.	76,196 − 56,456 = **19,740**	20.	88,067 − 34,980 = **53,087**	21.	23,999 − 21,938 = **2,061**	22.	74,665 − 43,883 = **30,782**	23.	76,486 − 56,758 = **19,728**	24.	35,348 − 12,340 = **23,008**
25.	32,675 − 27,456 = **5,219**	26.	87,906 − 56,945 = **30,961**	27.	63,921 − 56,712 = **7,209**								

32   CD-104320 • © Carson-Dellosa

Worksheet 2 (page 33)

Name _____ Date _____

Subtraction of Decimals

Total Problems: 33
Problems Correct: _____

Solve each problem. Regroup when necessary.

Don't Bat an Eye at Subtraction!

#		#		#		#		#		#	
1.	7.36 − 3.97 = **3.39**	2.	8.90 − 2.49 = **6.41**	3.	7.68 − 4.79 = **2.89**	4.	3.85 − 2.79 = **1.06**	5.	7.47 − 4.58 = **2.89**	6.	8.37 − 2.09 = **6.28**
7.	4.76 − 2.67 = **2.09**	8.	6.89 − 4.78 = **2.11**	9.	6.77 − 2.88 = **3.89**	10.	3.76 − 1.87 = **1.89**	11.	5.21 − 2.94 = **2.27**	12.	3.87 − 3.29 = **0.58**
13.	3.01 − 2.42 = **0.59**	14.	5.41 − 3.77 = **1.64**	15.	4.71 − 3.82 = **0.89**	16.	7.27 − 4.19 = **3.08**	17.	8.48 − 3.99 = **4.49**	18.	8.47 − 3.58 = **4.89**
19.	5.02 − 3.21 = **1.81**	20.	7.04 − 6.67 = **0.37**	21.	8.46 − 4.57 = **3.89**	22.	6.03 − 2.77 = **3.26**	23.	4.05 − 2.28 = **1.77**	24.	2.35 − 1.28 = **1.07**
25.	7.03 − 4.78 = **2.25**	26.	7.87 − 5.48 = **2.39**	27.	5.84 − 2.95 = **2.89**	28.	6.00 − 3.67 = **2.33**	29.	4.00 − 3.73 = **0.27**	30.	5.48 − 3.69 = **1.79**
31.	8.34 − 6.57 = **1.77**	32.	7.48 − 2.59 = **4.89**	33.	7.48 − 4.59 = **2.89**								

CD-104320 • © Carson-Dellosa   33

Worksheet 3 (page 34)

Name _____ Date _____

Subtraction of Decimals

Total Problems: 33
Problems Correct: _____

Solve each problem. Regroup when necessary.

You're Doing Swimmingly!

#		#		#		#		#		#	
1.	7.84 − 5.91 = **1.93**	2.	5.47 − 2.65 = **2.82**	3.	6.22 − 3.23 = **2.99**	4.	8.25 − 6.38 = **1.87**	5.	9.23 − 5.68 = **3.55**	6.	9.50 − 5.80 = **3.70**
7.	6.63 − 2.61 = **4.02**	8.	9.67 − 7.94 = **1.73**	9.	9.82 − 3.98 = **5.84**	10.	2.93 − 1.87 = **1.06**	11.	7.32 − 4.67 = **2.65**	12.	8.24 − 5.48 = **2.76**
13.	8.45 − 5.66 = **2.79**	14.	4.29 − 1.88 = **2.41**	15.	6.59 − 4.78 = **1.81**	16.	7.25 − 4.69 = **2.56**	17.	8.27 − 6.45 = **1.82**	18.	5.36 − 4.59 = **0.77**
19.	5.27 − 2.65 = **2.62**	20.	5.74 − 2.93 = **2.81**	21.	5.57 − 2.78 = **2.79**	22.	4.23 − 1.55 = **2.68**	23.	7.66 − 5.77 = **1.89**	24.	5.36 − 2.58 = **2.78**
25.	6.77 − 2.89 = **3.88**	26.	8.57 − 6.75 = **1.82**	27.	7.86 − 3.89 = **3.97**	28.	7.48 − 3.53 = **3.95**	29.	8.31 − 3.57 = **4.74**	30.	5.12 − 2.45 = **2.67**
31.	9.40 − 5.65 = **3.75**	32.	4.38 − 2.54 = **1.84**	33.	4.87 − 3.78 = **1.09**								

34   CD-104320 • © Carson-Dellosa

Worksheet 4 (page 35)

Name _____ Date _____

Subtraction of Fractions

Total Problems: 24
Problems Correct: _____

Solve each problem. Write each answer in its simplest form.

Fishing for Answers!

1. $\frac{5}{6} - \frac{4}{6} = \frac{1}{6}$
2. $\frac{4}{7} - \frac{2}{7} = \frac{2}{7}$
3. $\frac{3}{5} - \frac{2}{5} = \frac{1}{5}$
4. $\frac{10}{11} - \frac{5}{11} = \frac{5}{11}$
5. $\frac{5}{8} - \frac{1}{8} = \frac{1}{2}$
6. $\frac{4}{5} - \frac{3}{5} = \frac{1}{5}$

7. $\frac{3}{6} - \frac{2}{6} = \frac{1}{6}$
8. $\frac{3}{4} - \frac{2}{4} = \frac{1}{4}$
9. $\frac{7}{10} - \frac{2}{10} = \frac{1}{2}$
10. $\frac{7}{8} - \frac{4}{8} = \frac{3}{8}$
11. $\frac{1}{3} - \frac{1}{3} = 0$
12. $\frac{7}{8} - \frac{2}{8} = \frac{5}{8}$

13. $\frac{4}{9} - \frac{2}{9} = \frac{2}{9}$
14. $\frac{9}{11} - \frac{1}{11} = \frac{8}{11}$
15. $\frac{4}{10} - \frac{3}{10} = \frac{1}{10}$
16. $\frac{8}{12} - \frac{5}{12} = \frac{1}{4}$
17. $\frac{3}{8} - \frac{1}{8} = \frac{1}{4}$
18. $\frac{4}{7} - \frac{1}{7} = \frac{3}{7}$

19. $\frac{8}{9} - \frac{2}{9} = \frac{2}{3}$
20. $\frac{4}{5} - \frac{1}{5} = \frac{3}{5}$
21. $\frac{9}{12} - \frac{2}{12} = \frac{7}{12}$
22. $\frac{8}{11} - \frac{2}{11} = \frac{6}{11}$
23. $\frac{6}{7} - \frac{1}{7} = \frac{5}{7}$
24. $\frac{8}{10} - \frac{2}{10} = \frac{3}{5}$

CD-104320 • © Carson-Dellosa   35

Multiplication with the Factor 2

Name _____ Date _____

Total Problems: 33
Problems Correct: _____

Solve each problem.

Catch on to Multiplication!

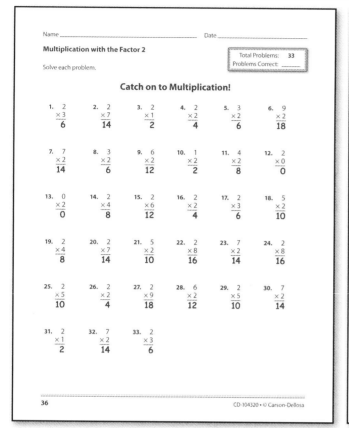

1. $2 \times 3 = 6$
2. $2 \times 7 = 14$
3. $2 \times 1 = 2$
4. $2 \times 2 = 4$
5. $3 \times 2 = 6$
6. $9 \times 2 = 18$
7. $7 \times 2 = 14$
8. $3 \times 2 = 6$
9. $6 \times 2 = 12$
10. $1 \times 2 = 2$
11. $4 \times 2 = 8$
12. $2 \times 0 = 0$
13. $0 \times 2 = 0$
14. $2 \times 4 = 8$
15. $2 \times 6 = 12$
16. $2 \times 2 = 4$
17. $2 \times 3 = 6$
18. $5 \times 2 = 10$
19. $2 \times 4 = 8$
20. $2 \times 7 = 14$
21. $5 \times 2 = 10$
22. $2 \times 8 = 16$
23. $7 \times 2 = 14$
24. $2 \times 8 = 16$
25. $2 \times 5 = 10$
26. $2 \times 2 = 4$
27. $2 \times 9 = 18$
28. $6 \times 2 = 12$
29. $2 \times 5 = 10$
30. $7 \times 2 = 14$
31. $2 \times 1 = 2$
32. $7 \times 2 = 14$
33. $2 \times 3 = 6$

36   CD-104320 • © Carson-Dellosa

Multiplication with Factors 0–2

Name _____ Date _____

Total Problems: 33
Problems Correct: _____

Solve each problem.

You've Got It!

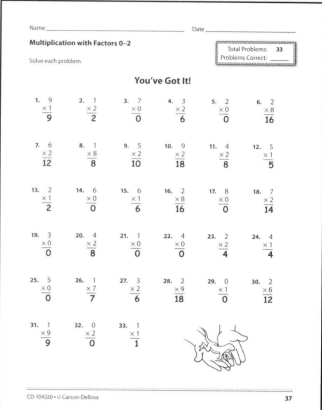

1. $9 \times 1 = 9$
2. $1 \times 2 = 2$
3. $7 \times 0 = 0$
4. $3 \times 2 = 6$
5. $2 \times 0 = 0$
6. $2 \times 8 = 16$
7. $6 \times 2 = 12$
8. $1 \times 8 = 8$
9. $5 \times 2 = 10$
10. $9 \times 2 = 18$
11. $4 \times 2 = 8$
12. $5 \times 1 = 5$
13. $2 \times 1 = 2$
14. $6 \times 0 = 0$
15. $6 \times 1 = 6$
16. $2 \times 8 = 16$
17. $8 \times 0 = 0$
18. $7 \times 2 = 14$
19. $3 \times 0 = 0$
20. $4 \times 2 = 8$
21. $1 \times 0 = 0$
22. $4 \times 0 = 0$
23. $2 \times 2 = 4$
24. $4 \times 1 = 4$
25. $5 \times 0 = 0$
26. $1 \times 7 = 7$
27. $3 \times 2 = 6$
28. $2 \times 9 = 18$
29. $0 \times 1 = 0$
30. $2 \times 6 = 12$
31. $1 \times 9 = 9$
32. $0 \times 2 = 0$
33. $1 \times 1 = 1$

CD-104320 • © Carson-Dellosa   37

Multiplication with the Factor 3

Name _____ Date _____

Total Problems: 33
Problems Correct: _____

Solve each problem.

Roll Through Multiplication!

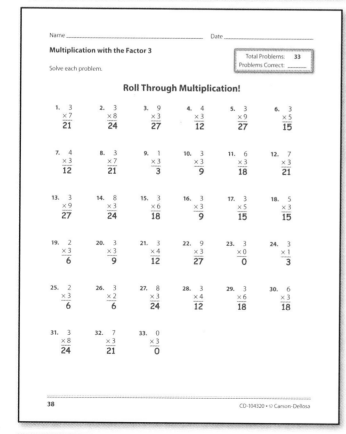

1. $3 \times 7 = 21$
2. $3 \times 8 = 24$
3. $9 \times 3 = 27$
4. $4 \times 3 = 12$
5. $3 \times 9 = 27$
6. $3 \times 5 = 15$
7. $4 \times 3 = 12$
8. $3 \times 7 = 21$
9. $1 \times 3 = 3$
10. $3 \times 3 = 9$
11. $6 \times 3 = 18$
12. $7 \times 3 = 21$
13. $3 \times 9 = 27$
14. $8 \times 3 = 24$
15. $3 \times 6 = 18$
16. $3 \times 3 = 9$
17. $3 \times 5 = 15$
18. $5 \times 3 = 15$
19. $2 \times 3 = 6$
20. $3 \times 3 = 9$
21. $3 \times 4 = 12$
22. $9 \times 3 = 27$
23. $3 \times 0 = 0$
24. $3 \times 1 = 3$
25. $2 \times 3 = 6$
26. $3 \times 2 = 6$
27. $8 \times 3 = 24$
28. $3 \times 4 = 12$
29. $3 \times 6 = 18$
30. $6 \times 3 = 18$
31. $3 \times 8 = 24$
32. $7 \times 3 = 21$
33. $0 \times 3 = 0$

38   CD-104320 • © Carson-Dellosa

Multiplication with Factors 2 and 3

Name _____ Date _____

Total Problems: 33
Problems Correct: _____

Solve each problem.

You're on a Roll!

1. $3 \times 9 = 27$
2. $3 \times 0 = 0$
3. $2 \times 1 = 2$
4. $3 \times 2 = 6$
5. $8 \times 3 = 24$
6. $3 \times 7 = 21$
7. $3 \times 4 = 12$
8. $3 \times 8 = 24$
9. $4 \times 3 = 12$
10. $2 \times 2 = 4$
11. $2 \times 3 = 6$
12. $2 \times 6 = 12$
13. $2 \times 0 = 0$
14. $1 \times 2 = 2$
15. $0 \times 3 = 0$
16. $3 \times 5 = 15$
17. $5 \times 2 = 10$
18. $2 \times 7 = 14$
19. $3 \times 3 = 9$
20. $9 \times 3 = 27$
21. $3 \times 6 = 18$
22. $4 \times 2 = 8$
23. $5 \times 3 = 15$
24. $7 \times 3 = 21$
25. $6 \times 2 = 12$
26. $6 \times 3 = 18$
27. $3 \times 3 = 9$
28. $7 \times 2 = 14$
29. $2 \times 8 = 16$
30. $2 \times 9 = 18$
31. $9 \times 2 = 18$
32. $8 \times 2 = 16$
33. $2 \times 4 = 8$

CD-104320 • © Carson-Dellosa   39

Multiplication with the Factor 4

Name _____ Date _____

Total Problems: **33**
Problems Correct: _____

Solve each problem.

You're on Your Way Up!

#		#		#		#		#		#	
1.	9 ×4 = 36	2.	4 ×8 = 32	3.	7 ×4 = 28	4.	4 ×7 = 28	5.	6 ×4 = 24	6.	4 ×5 = 20
7.	4 ×2 = 8	8.	3 ×4 = 12	9.	4 ×3 = 12	10.	4 ×1 = 4	11.	8 ×4 = 32	12.	4 ×9 = 36
13.	4 ×6 = 24	14.	1 ×4 = 4	15.	4 ×2 = 8	16.	2 ×4 = 8	17.	4 ×4 = 16	18.	7 ×4 = 28
19.	4 ×0 = 0	20.	4 ×9 = 36	21.	7 ×4 = 28	22.	4 ×6 = 24	23.	4 ×5 = 20	24.	4 ×9 = 36
25.	4 ×4 = 16	26.	4 ×8 = 32	27.	0 ×4 = 0	28.	4 ×5 = 20	29.	4 ×7 = 28	30.	5 ×4 = 20
31.	8 ×4 = 32	32.	9 ×4 = 36	33.	4 ×9 = 36						

Multiplication with Factors 2–4

Name _____ Date _____

Total Problems: **33**
Problems Correct: _____

Solve each problem.

Get a Leg Up on Math!

#		#		#		#		#		#	
1.	7 ×4 = 28	2.	8 ×4 = 32	3.	4 ×9 = 36	4.	5 ×4 = 20	5.	2 ×3 = 6	6.	4 ×2 = 8
7.	3 ×2 = 6	8.	3 ×1 = 3	9.	6 ×2 = 12	10.	3 ×5 = 15	11.	8 ×3 = 24	12.	8 ×4 = 32
13.	3 ×3 = 9	14.	4 ×4 = 16	15.	5 ×2 = 10	16.	6 ×4 = 24	17.	12 ×2 = 24	18.	7 ×3 = 21
19.	3 ×6 = 18	20.	8 ×3 = 24	21.	3 ×3 = 9	22.	2 ×9 = 18	23.	1 ×4 = 4	24.	3 ×2 = 6
25.	2 ×2 = 4	26.	2 ×4 = 8	27.	9 ×4 = 36	28.	1 ×3 = 3	29.	2 ×8 = 16	30.	3 ×5 = 15
31.	1 ×4 = 4	32.	2 ×7 = 14	33.	4 ×5 = 20						

Multiplication with the Factor 5

Name _____ Date _____

Total Problems: **33**
Problems Correct: _____

Solve each problem.

The Sweet Rewards of Math!

#		#		#		#		#		#	
1.	5 ×7 = 35	2.	5 ×9 = 45	3.	6 ×5 = 30	4.	0 ×5 = 0	5.	5 ×8 = 40	6.	5 ×0 = 0
7.	2 ×5 = 10	8.	7 ×5 = 35	9.	9 ×5 = 45	10.	5 ×3 = 15	11.	5 ×6 = 30	12.	5 ×7 = 35
13.	2 ×5 = 10	14.	5 ×5 = 25	15.	5 ×4 = 20	16.	4 ×5 = 20	17.	5 ×2 = 10	18.	9 ×5 = 45
19.	4 ×5 = 20	20.	8 ×5 = 40	21.	1 ×5 = 5	22.	5 ×5 = 25	23.	3 ×5 = 15	24.	5 ×6 = 30
25.	5 ×8 = 40	26.	5 ×4 = 20	27.	6 ×5 = 30	28.	5 ×5 = 25	29.	5 ×3 = 15	30.	5 ×1 = 5
31.	5 ×2 = 10	32.	5 ×9 = 45	33.	9 ×5 = 45						

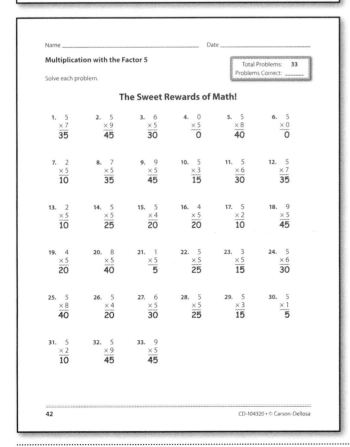

Multiplication with Factors 4 and 5

Name _____ Date _____

Total Problems: **33**
Problems Correct: _____

Solve each problem.

Be a Busy Bee!

#		#		#		#		#		#	
1.	5 ×6 = 30	2.	5 ×7 = 35	3.	5 ×8 = 40	4.	8 ×5 = 40	5.	2 ×5 = 10	6.	3 ×5 = 15
7.	4 ×8 = 32	8.	4 ×2 = 8	9.	5 ×5 = 25	10.	8 ×4 = 32	11.	4 ×9 = 36	12.	4 ×1 = 4
13.	5 ×3 = 15	14.	0 ×4 = 0	15.	7 ×5 = 35	16.	9 ×5 = 45	17.	3 ×4 = 12	18.	5 ×5 = 25
19.	7 ×4 = 28	20.	5 ×2 = 10	21.	1 ×5 = 5	22.	4 ×7 = 28	23.	5 ×9 = 45	24.	5 ×3 = 15
25.	6 ×4 = 24	26.	4 ×2 = 8	27.	1 ×4 = 4	28.	4 ×3 = 12	29.	6 ×5 = 30	30.	5 ×4 = 20
31.	9 ×4 = 36	32.	4 ×5 = 20	33.	4 ×6 = 24						

Name _____ Date _____

Multiplication with Factors 2–5

Solve each problem.

Total Problems: **33**
Problems Correct: _____

Swinging Through Multiplication!

1. 2 ×5 **10**	2. 5 ×8 **40**	3. 5 ×3 **15**	4. 8 ×4 **32**	5. 3 ×4 **12**	6. 7 ×2 **14**
7. 7 ×5 **35**	8. 1 ×4 **4**	9. 3 ×5 **15**	10. 2 ×2 **4**	11. 8 ×3 **24**	12. 4 ×3 **12**
13. 4 ×6 **24**	14. 5 ×2 **10**	15. 4 ×5 **20**	16. 2 ×9 **18**	17. 5 ×5 **25**	18. 5 ×6 **30**
19. 4 ×2 **8**	20. 4 ×9 **36**	21. 9 ×3 **27**	22. 4 ×4 **16**	23. 3 ×7 **21**	24. 8 ×2 **16**
25. 6 ×2 **12**	26. 3 ×6 **18**	27. 2 ×4 **8**	28. 4 ×7 **28**	29. 3 ×2 **6**	30. 9 ×5 **45**
31. 5 ×1 **5**	32. 2 ×3 **6**	33. 3 ×1 **3**			

44   CD-104320 • © Carson-Dellosa

Name _____ Date _____

Multiplication with the Factor 6

Solve each problem.

Total Problems: **33**
Problems Correct: _____

Hanging Around with Math!

1. 8 ×6 **48**	2. 2 ×6 **12**	3. 7 ×6 **42**	4. 6 ×5 **30**	5. 5 ×6 **30**	6. 6 ×7 **42**
7. 7 ×6 **48**	8. 6 ×3 **18**	9. 6 ×8 **48**	10. 6 ×4 **24**	11. 5 ×6 **30**	12. 6 ×0 **0**
13. 8 ×6 **48**	14. 4 ×6 **24**	15. 2 ×6 **12**	16. 6 ×6 **36**	17. 3 ×6 **18**	18. 6 ×3 **18**
19. 6 ×4 **24**	20. 6 ×9 **54**	21. 7 ×6 **42**	22. 6 ×1 **6**	23. 6 ×2 **12**	24. 6 ×9 **54**
25. 6 ×6 **36**	26. 6 ×3 **18**	27. 6 ×5 **30**	28. 9 ×6 **54**	29. 6 ×8 **48**	30. 1 ×6 **6**
31. 3 ×6 **18**	32. 6 ×6 **36**	33. 9 ×6 **54**			

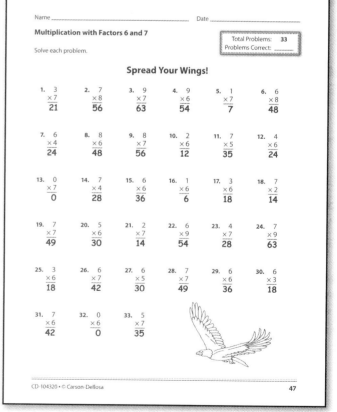

CD-104320 • © Carson-Dellosa   45

Name _____ Date _____

Multiplication with the Factor 7

Solve each problem.

Total Problems: **33**
Problems Correct: _____

Soar Through Multiplication!

1. 0 ×7 **0**	2. 8 ×7 **56**	3. 2 ×7 **14**	4. 7 ×7 **49**	5. 7 ×5 **35**	6. 7 ×8 **56**
7. 7 ×7 **49**	8. 7 ×2 **14**	9. 9 ×7 **63**	10. 7 ×9 **63**	11. 4 ×7 **28**	12. 1 ×7 **7**
13. 8 ×7 **56**	14. 3 ×7 **21**	15. 6 ×7 **42**	16. 7 ×4 **28**	17. 5 ×7 **35**	18. 4 ×7 **28**
19. 5 ×7 **35**	20. 7 ×4 **28**	21. 7 ×0 **0**	22. 7 ×2 **14**	23. 7 ×8 **56**	24. 7 ×9 **63**
25. 2 ×7 **14**	26. 7 ×6 **42**	27. 7 ×2 **14**	28. 6 ×7 **42**	29. 7 ×3 **21**	30. 7 ×5 **35**
31. 7 ×6 **42**	32. 7 ×7 **49**	33. 7 ×3 **21**			

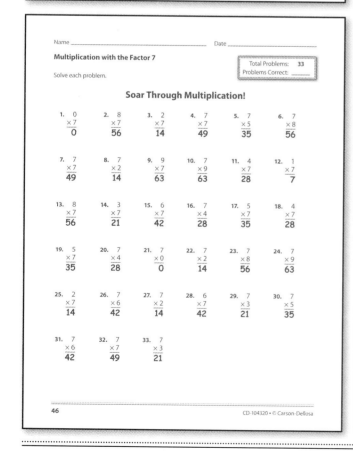

46   CD-104320 • © Carson-Dellosa

Name _____ Date _____

Multiplication with Factors 6 and 7

Solve each problem.

Total Problems: **33**
Problems Correct: _____

Spread Your Wings!

1. 3 ×7 **21**	2. 7 ×8 **56**	3. 9 ×7 **63**	4. 9 ×6 **54**	5. 1 ×7 **7**	6. 6 ×8 **48**
7. 6 ×4 **24**	8. 8 ×6 **48**	9. 8 ×7 **56**	10. 2 ×6 **12**	11. 7 ×5 **35**	12. 4 ×6 **24**
13. 0 ×7 **0**	14. 7 ×4 **28**	15. 6 ×6 **36**	16. 1 ×6 **6**	17. 3 ×6 **18**	18. 7 ×2 **14**
19. 7 ×7 **49**	20. 5 ×6 **30**	21. 2 ×7 **14**	22. 6 ×9 **54**	23. 4 ×7 **28**	24. 7 ×9 **63**
25. 3 ×6 **18**	26. 6 ×7 **42**	27. 6 ×5 **30**	28. 7 ×7 **49**	29. 6 ×6 **36**	30. 6 ×3 **18**
31. 7 ×6 **42**	32. 0 ×6 **0**	33. 5 ×7 **35**			

CD-104320 • © Carson-Dellosa   47

Worksheet (page 48)

Name _____ Date _____

Multiplication with the Factor 8

Total Problems:	33
Problems Correct:	_____

Solve each problem.

Way to Go!

1. 8 ×9 **72**	2. 7 ×8 **56**	3. 4 ×8 **32**	4. 0 ×8 **0**	5. 8 ×6 **48**	6. 8 ×0 **0**
7. 8 ×8 **64**	8. 1 ×8 **8**	9. 9 ×8 **72**	10. 2 ×8 **16**	11. 8 ×3 **24**	12. 8 ×4 **32**
13. 6 ×8 **48**	14. 8 ×5 **40**	15. 5 ×8 **40**	16. 2 ×8 **16**	17. 9 ×8 **72**	18. 8 ×8 **64**
19. 4 ×8 **32**	20. 8 ×3 **24**	21. 8 ×2 **16**	22. 2 ×8 **16**	23. 8 ×5 **40**	24. 3 ×8 **24**
25. 8 ×2 **16**	26. 8 ×9 **72**	27. 9 ×8 **72**	28. 8 ×7 **56**	29. 8 ×1 **8**	30. 8 ×6 **48**
31. 8 ×7 **56**	32. 8 ×4 **32**	33. 8 ×5 **40**			

Worksheet (page 49)

Name _____ Date _____

Multiplication with the Factor 9

Total Problems:	33
Problems Correct:	_____

Solve each problem.

Nice Job!

1. 5 ×9 **45**	2. 9 ×3 **27**	3. 9 ×9 **81**	4. 9 ×1 **9**	5. 0 ×9 **0**	6. 9 ×9 **81**
7. 9 ×8 **72**	8. 5 ×9 **45**	9. 9 ×2 **18**	10. 9 ×8 **72**	11. 3 ×9 **27**	12. 9 ×6 **54**
13. 9 ×9 **81**	14. 9 ×4 **36**	15. 5 ×9 **45**	16. 6 ×9 **54**	17. 9 ×2 **18**	18. 2 ×9 **18**
19. 9 ×5 **45**	20. 9 ×9 **81**	21. 3 ×9 **27**	22. 8 ×9 **72**	23. 9 ×7 **63**	24. 9 ×0 **0**
25. 9 ×3 **27**	26. 9 ×7 **63**	27. 1 ×9 **9**	28. 9 ×4 **36**	29. 2 ×9 **18**	30. 4 ×9 **36**
31. 8 ×9 **72**	32. 4 ×9 **36**	33. 6 ×9 **54**			

Worksheet (page 50)

Name _____ Date _____

Multiplication with Factors 8 and 9

Total Problems:	33
Problems Correct:	_____

Solve each problem.

Put Your Mind to It!

1. 9 ×7 **63**	2. 4 ×8 **32**	3. 9 ×5 **45**	4. 6 ×8 **48**	5. 8 ×2 **16**	6. 8 ×9 **72**
7. 9 ×3 **27**	8. 8 ×5 **40**	9. 9 ×2 **18**	10. 8 ×3 **24**	11. 7 ×9 **63**	12. 8 ×7 **56**
13. 6 ×9 **54**	14. 8 ×6 **48**	15. 9 ×4 **36**	16. 7 ×8 **56**	17. 1 ×8 **8**	18. 9 ×6 **54**
19. 3 ×8 **24**	20. 2 ×9 **18**	21. 0 ×8 **0**	22. 4 ×9 **36**	23. 9 ×9 **81**	24. 8 ×8 **64**
25. 5 ×8 **40**	26. 0 ×9 **0**	27. 5 ×9 **45**	28. 8 ×4 **32**	29. 3 ×9 **27**	30. 9 ×9 **81**
31. 8 ×9 **72**	32. 9 ×8 **72**	33. 1 ×9 **9**			

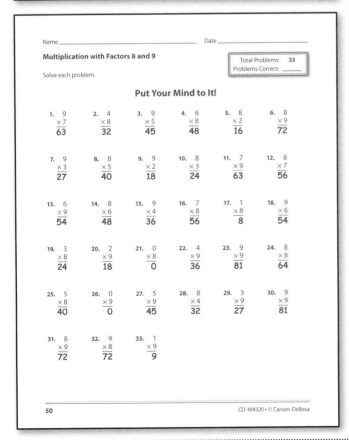

Worksheet (page 51)

Name _____ Date _____

Multiplication with Factors 6–9

Total Problems:	33
Problems Correct:	_____

Solve each problem.

Yes, You Can!

1. 4 ×9 **36**	2. 6 ×8 **48**	3. 6 ×7 **42**	4. 8 ×5 **40**	5. 7 ×6 **42**	6. 9 ×7 **63**
7. 2 ×9 **18**	8. 7 ×7 **49**	9. 6 ×2 **12**	10. 8 ×7 **56**	11. 9 ×8 **72**	12. 6 ×7 **42**
13. 8 ×8 **64**	14. 7 ×8 **56**	15. 6 ×6 **36**	16. 2 ×7 **14**	17. 5 ×9 **45**	18. 9 ×3 **27**
19. 1 ×6 **6**	20. 3 ×8 **24**	21. 7 ×5 **35**	22. 4 ×8 **32**	23. 3 ×6 **18**	24. 9 ×8 **72**
25. 4 ×6 **24**	26. 7 ×4 **28**	27. 1 ×8 **8**	28. 5 ×6 **30**	29. 9 ×9 **81**	30. 3 ×7 **21**
31. 9 ×1 **9**	32. 7 ×9 **63**	33. 8 ×6 **48**			

Name _____ Date _____

Multiplication with Factors 2–9

Total Problems: **33**
Problems Correct: _____

Solve each problem.

Keep on Marching!

| 1. | 8
× 5
40 | 2. | 6
× 4
24 | 3. | 5
× 5
25 | 4. | 9
× 5
45 | 5. | 4
× 4
16 | 6. | 6
× 3
18 |

7. 7 × 4 = **28** 8. 7 × 3 = **21** 9. 3 × 8 = **24** 10. 6 × 2 = **12** 11. 9 × 3 = **27** 12. 5 × 3 = **15**

13. 5 × 4 = **20** 14. 1 × 2 = **2** 15. 5 × 6 = **30** 16. 1 × 4 = **4** 17. 4 × 5 = **20** 18. 2 × 3 = **6**

19. 8 × 2 = **16** 20. 9 × 4 = **36** 21. 4 × 3 = **12** 22. 4 × 2 = **8** 23. 4 × 8 = **32** 24. 7 × 2 = **14**

25. 1 × 5 = **5** 26. 3 × 7 = **21** 27. 3 × 5 = **15** 28. 3 × 4 = **12** 29. 3 × 2 = **6** 30. 2 × 4 = **8**

31. 5 × 2 = **10** 32. 3 × 3 = **9** 33. 9 × 2 = **18**

52   CD-104320 • © Carson-Dellosa

Name _____ Date _____

Multiplication with Factors 2–9

Total Problems: **33**
Problems Correct: _____

Solve each problem.

Keep Up the Hard Work!

1. 2 × 7 = **14** 2. 7 × 5 = **35** 3. 5 × 6 = **30** 4. 2 × 7 = **14** 5. 4 × 8 = **32** 6. 7 × 6 = **42**

7. 4 × 9 = **36** 8. 7 × 3 = **21** 9. 6 × 6 = **36** 10. 5 × 9 = **45** 11. 4 × 2 = **8** 12. 2 × 6 = **12**

13. 3 × 6 = **18** 14. 8 × 7 = **56** 15. 8 × 6 = **48** 16. 5 × 7 = **35** 17. 1 × 5 = **5** 18. 4 × 5 = **20**

19. 8 × 5 = **40** 20. 4 × 3 = **12** 21. 6 × 5 = **30** 22. 7 × 7 = **49** 23. 9 × 6 = **54** 24. 7 × 9 = **63**

25. 0 × 6 = **0** 26. 0 × 7 = **0** 27. 5 × 5 = **25** 28. 6 × 7 = **42** 29. 4 × 4 = **16** 30. 6 × 4 = **24**

31. 4 × 7 = **28** 32. 2 × 5 = **10** 33. 1 × 3 = **3**

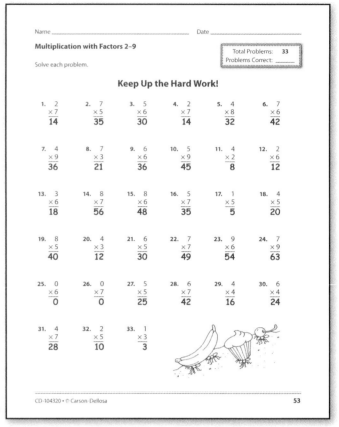

CD-104320 • © Carson-Dellosa   53

Name _____ Date _____

Multiplication with Factors 2–9

Total Problems: **33**
Problems Correct: _____

Solve each problem.

Dive Deep into Multiplication!

1. 8 × 7 = **56** 2. 3 × 7 = **21** 3. 6 × 6 = **36** 4. 4 × 7 = **28** 5. 6 × 7 = **42** 6. 6 × 8 = **48**

7. 8 × 8 = **64** 8. 6 × 7 = **42** 9. 5 × 0 = **0** 10. 2 × 8 = **16** 11. 3 × 5 = **15** 12. 3 × 6 = **18**

13. 5 × 5 = **25** 14. 1 × 7 = **7** 15. 7 × 6 = **42** 16. 2 × 7 = **14** 17. 4 × 6 = **24** 18. 9 × 7 = **63**

19. 7 × 7 = **49** 20. 3 × 8 = **24** 21. 5 × 7 = **35** 22. 8 × 6 = **48** 23. 2 × 6 = **12** 24. 4 × 5 = **20**

25. 9 × 8 = **72** 26. 7 × 5 = **35** 27. 8 × 5 = **40** 28. 5 × 5 = **25** 29. 4 × 8 = **32** 30. 7 × 8 = **56**

31. 5 × 9 = **45** 32. 9 × 6 = **54** 33. 5 × 8 = **40**

54   CD-104320 • © Carson-Dellosa

Name _____ Date _____

Multiplication with Factors 2–9

Total Problems: **33**
Problems Correct: _____

Solve each problem.

Slide into Multiplication!

1. 9 × 4 = **36** 2. 6 × 9 = **54** 3. 5 × 6 = **30** 4. 5 × 3 = **15** 5. 7 × 9 = **63** 6. 8 × 3 = **24**

7. 6 × 7 = **42** 8. 4 × 5 = **20** 9. 4 × 2 = **8** 10. 4 × 4 = **16** 11. 9 × 7 = **63** 12. 8 × 8 = **64**

13. 7 × 2 = **14** 14. 8 × 6 = **48** 15. 6 × 8 = **48** 16. 4 × 6 = **24** 17. 8 × 4 = **32** 18. 6 × 3 = **18**

19. 8 × 5 = **40** 20. 9 × 8 = **72** 21. 4 × 3 = **12** 22. 8 × 9 = **72** 23. 6 × 5 = **30** 24. 9 × 2 = **18**

25. 7 × 4 = **28** 26. 5 × 9 = **45** 27. 5 × 7 = **35** 28. 7 × 3 = **21** 29. 3 × 7 = **21** 30. 7 × 8 = **56**

31. 5 × 7 = **35** 32. 6 × 6 = **36** 33. 8 × 2 = **16**

CD-104320 • © Carson-Dellosa   55

Answer Key

Page 56

Name _____ Date _____

Multiplication with Factors 8–10

Total Problems:	33
Problems Correct:	_____

Solve each problem. Regroup when necessary.

To the Top!

1. 8 ×5 = 40	2. 8 ×9 = 72	3. 10 ×4 = 40	4. 9 ×9 = 81	5. 4 ×8 = 32	6. 10 ×8 = 80
7. 10 ×10 = 100	8. 7 ×9 = 63	9. 11 ×8 = 88	10. 9 ×8 = 72	11. 7 ×8 = 56	12. 4 ×9 = 36
13. 3 ×8 = 24	14. 10 ×5 = 50	15. 5 ×9 = 45	16. 3 ×9 = 27	17. 10 ×5 = 50	18. 10 ×9 = 90
19. 12 ×8 = 96	20. 1 ×8 = 8	21. 12 ×8 = 96	22. 10 ×7 = 70	23. 10 ×1 = 10	24. 6 ×8 = 48
25. 10 ×9 = 90	26. 11 ×10 = 110	27. 10 ×2 = 20	28. 12 ×9 = 108	29. 10 ×8 = 80	30. 12 ×8 = 96
31. 9 ×1 = 9	32. 8 ×5 = 40	33. 10 ×9 = 90			

Page 57

Name _____ Date _____

Multiplication with Factors 11 and 12

Total Problems:	33
Problems Correct:	_____

Solve each problem. Regroup when necessary.

Climb High with Multiplication!

1. 12 ×7 = 84	2. 11 ×6 = 66	3. 12 ×7 = 84	4. 12 ×6 = 72	5. 11 ×11 = 121	6. 11 ×2 = 22
7. 11 ×10 = 110	8. 12 ×9 = 108	9. 11 ×10 = 110	10. 12 ×2 = 24	11. 12 ×10 = 120	12. 12 ×12 = 144
13. 11 ×9 = 99	14. 12 ×9 = 108	15. 11 ×8 = 88	16. 11 ×3 = 33	17. 11 ×8 = 88	18. 12 ×10 = 120
19. 11 ×9 = 99	20. 12 ×12 = 144	21. 12 ×11 = 132	22. 12 ×1 = 12	23. 12 ×1 = 12	24. 12 ×8 = 96
25. 12 ×3 = 36	26. 11 ×7 = 77	27. 12 ×4 = 48	28. 12 ×6 = 72	29. 11 ×9 = 99	30. 11 ×4 = 44
31. 12 ×8 = 96	32. 11 ×7 = 77	33. 11 ×5 = 55			

Page 58

Name _____ Date _____

Two-Digit by One-Digit Multiplication

Total Problems:	33
Problems Correct:	_____

Solve each problem.

Fan the Flame of Multiplication!

1. 32 ×3 = 96	2. 23 ×2 = 46	3. 20 ×4 = 80	4. 24 ×2 = 48	5. 44 ×2 = 88	6. 13 ×3 = 39
7. 44 ×2 = 88	8. 22 ×2 = 44	9. 33 ×3 = 99	10. 21 ×4 = 84	11. 21 ×3 = 63	12. 31 ×3 = 93
13. 13 ×3 = 39	14. 31 ×2 = 62	15. 57 ×1 = 57	16. 14 ×2 = 28	17. 30 ×3 = 90	18. 41 ×2 = 82
19. 34 ×2 = 68	20. 21 ×3 = 63	21. 10 ×7 = 70	22. 22 ×4 = 88	23. 33 ×2 = 66	24. 11 ×4 = 44
25. 40 ×2 = 80	26. 43 ×2 = 86	27. 22 ×4 = 88	28. 12 ×1 = 12	29. 12 ×4 = 48	30. 33 ×2 = 66
31. 22 ×4 = 88	32. 11 ×5 = 55	33. 44 ×2 = 88			

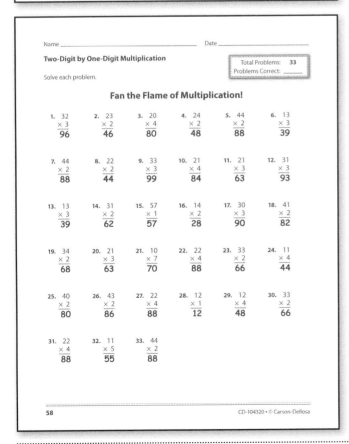

Page 59

Name _____ Date _____

Two-Digit by One-Digit Multiplication with Regrouping

Total Problems:	33
Problems Correct:	_____

Solve each problem. Regroup when necessary.

Keep the Fire Going!

1. 16 ×5 = 80	2. 15 ×7 = 105	3. 28 ×3 = 84	4. 24 ×4 = 96	5. 26 ×4 = 104	6. 47 ×2 = 94
7. 19 ×4 = 76	8. 19 ×5 = 95	9. 38 ×2 = 76	10. 45 ×4 = 180	11. 19 ×6 = 114	12. 36 ×3 = 108
13. 14 ×7 = 98	14. 47 ×2 = 94	15. 66 ×3 = 198	16. 53 ×5 = 265	17. 29 ×4 = 116	18. 16 ×5 = 80
19. 23 ×4 = 92	20. 13 ×6 = 78	21. 67 ×5 = 335	22. 14 ×5 = 70	23. 13 ×7 = 91	24. 29 ×2 = 58
25. 32 ×5 = 160	26. 12 ×8 = 96	27. 13 ×4 = 52	28. 35 ×8 = 280	29. 47 ×3 = 141	30. 27 ×4 = 108
31. 28 ×5 = 140	32. 25 ×3 = 75	33. 14 ×4 = 56			

Worksheet 1 (page 60)

Name _____ Date _____

Two-Digit by One-Digit Multiplication with Regrouping

Solve each problem. Regroup when necessary.

Total Problems: **33**
Problems Correct: _____

Get to Know Math!

1. 45 × 2 = 90	2. 56 × 4 = 224	3. 34 × 3 = 102	4. 57 × 4 = 228	5. 28 × 3 = 84	6. 46 × 6 = 276
7. 39 × 6 = 234	8. 19 × 8 = 152	9. 36 × 6 = 216	10. 76 × 5 = 380	11. 44 × 5 = 220	12. 75 × 2 = 150
13. 27 × 6 = 162	14. 22 × 9 = 198	15. 83 × 6 = 498	16. 87 × 2 = 174	17. 37 × 3 = 111	18. 49 × 7 = 343
19. 74 × 3 = 222	20. 37 × 6 = 222	21. 53 × 5 = 265	22. 68 × 4 = 272	23. 38 × 4 = 152	24. 77 × 8 = 616
25. 63 × 7 = 441	26. 59 × 4 = 236	27. 42 × 7 = 294	28. 55 × 3 = 165	29. 57 × 3 = 171	30. 69 × 2 = 138
31. 59 × 2 = 118	32. 22 × 8 = 176	33. 57 × 8 = 456			

Worksheet 2 (page 61)

Name _____ Date _____

Two-Digit by One-Digit Multiplication with Regrouping

Solve each problem. Regroup when necessary.

Total Problems: **33**
Problems Correct: _____

Math Is Your Friend!

1. 34 × 3 = 102	2. 35 × 3 = 105	3. 13 × 5 = 65	4. 26 × 3 = 78	5. 15 × 3 = 45	6. 28 × 4 = 112
7. 36 × 2 = 72	8. 24 × 3 = 72	9. 15 × 7 = 105	10. 26 × 3 = 78	11. 17 × 7 = 119	12. 28 × 3 = 84
13. 36 × 3 = 108	14. 25 × 4 = 100	15. 14 × 7 = 98	16. 13 × 7 = 91	17. 35 × 2 = 70	18. 19 × 5 = 95
19. 14 × 5 = 70	20. 17 × 6 = 102	21. 15 × 6 = 90	22. 36 × 6 = 216	23. 15 × 3 = 45	24. 18 × 7 = 126
25. 12 × 6 = 72	26. 28 × 4 = 112	27. 37 × 3 = 111	28. 24 × 4 = 96	29. 33 × 4 = 132	30. 44 × 3 = 132
31. 23 × 4 = 92	32. 35 × 3 = 105	33. 28 × 2 = 56			

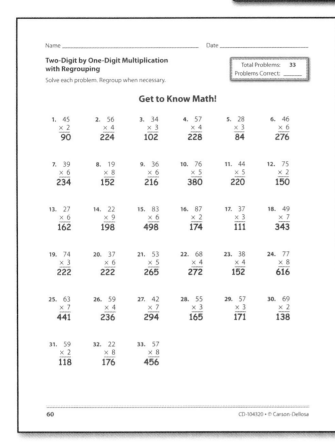

Worksheet 3 (page 62)

Name _____ Date _____

Two-Digit by One-Digit Multiplication with Regrouping

Solve each problem. Regroup when necessary.

Total Problems: **33**
Problems Correct: _____

Discover Multiplication!

1. 58 × 6 = 348	2. 82 × 6 = 492	3. 32 × 7 = 224	4. 27 × 6 = 162	5. 45 × 2 = 90	6. 28 × 5 = 140
7. 66 × 7 = 462	8. 83 × 5 = 415	9. 77 × 8 = 616	10. 57 × 8 = 456	11. 43 × 9 = 387	12. 86 × 5 = 430
13. 74 × 7 = 518	14. 69 × 2 = 138	15. 28 × 4 = 112	16. 54 × 7 = 378	17. 64 × 7 = 448	18. 36 × 6 = 216
19. 42 × 3 = 126	20. 54 × 4 = 216	21. 63 × 6 = 378	22. 87 × 2 = 174	23. 46 × 7 = 322	24. 49 × 5 = 245
25. 36 × 2 = 72	26. 38 × 9 = 342	27. 44 × 3 = 132	28. 55 × 4 = 220	29. 33 × 8 = 264	30. 87 × 3 = 261
31. 47 × 4 = 188	32. 78 × 2 = 156	33. 65 × 5 = 325			

Worksheet 4 (page 63)

Name _____ Date _____

Two-Digit by One-Digit Multiplication with Regrouping

Solve each problem. Regroup when necessary.

Total Problems: **33**
Problems Correct: _____

Explore Multiplication!

1. 78 × 2 = 156	2. 65 × 2 = 130	3. 68 × 2 = 136	4. 36 × 4 = 144	5. 43 × 5 = 215	6. 59 × 2 = 118
7. 46 × 5 = 230	8. 63 × 5 = 315	9. 55 × 2 = 110	10. 48 × 7 = 336	11. 49 × 8 = 392	12. 64 × 7 = 448
13. 67 × 3 = 201	14. 47 × 4 = 188	15. 39 × 4 = 156	16. 82 × 6 = 492	17. 73 × 4 = 292	18. 37 × 4 = 148
19. 27 × 5 = 135	20. 36 × 4 = 144	21. 57 × 2 = 114	22. 74 × 8 = 592	23. 68 × 2 = 136	24. 58 × 3 = 174
25. 64 × 6 = 384	26. 37 × 5 = 185	27. 46 × 5 = 230	28. 48 × 5 = 240	29. 77 × 4 = 308	30. 44 × 8 = 352
31. 83 × 5 = 415	32. 48 × 4 = 192	33. 75 × 2 = 150			

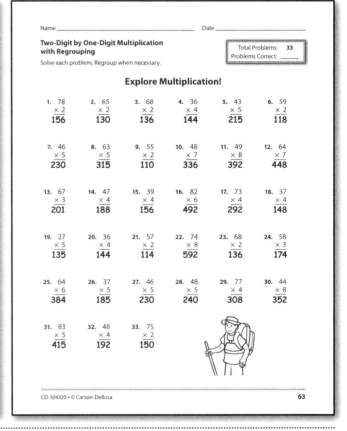

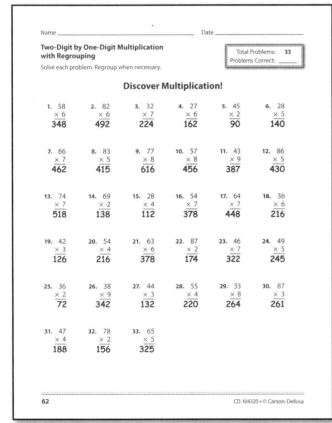

Worksheet 1 (page 64)

Name _____ Date _____

Two-Digit by One-Digit Multiplication with Regrouping

Total Problems:	33
Problems Correct:	_____

Solve each problem. Regroup when necessary.

Three Cheers for Multiplication!

1. 57 × 7 = 399	2. 58 × 2 = 116	3. 73 × 4 = 292	4. 17 × 6 = 102	5. 97 × 2 = 194	6. 68 × 3 = 204
7. 63 × 5 = 315	8. 66 × 2 = 132	9. 18 × 9 = 162	10. 65 × 5 = 325	11. 49 × 5 = 245	12. 73 × 5 = 365
13. 59 × 3 = 177	14. 39 × 2 = 78	15. 44 × 4 = 176	16. 78 × 6 = 468	17. 48 × 6 = 288	18. 58 × 8 = 464
19. 85 × 4 = 340	20. 99 × 4 = 396	21. 55 × 2 = 110	22. 84 × 4 = 336	23. 49 × 5 = 245	24. 69 × 3 = 207
25. 88 × 8 = 704	26. 46 × 3 = 138	27. 48 × 3 = 144	28. 89 × 3 = 267	29. 74 × 4 = 296	30. 14 × 3 = 42
31. 42 × 7 = 294	32. 78 × 8 = 624	33. 49 × 7 = 343			

64   CD-104320 • © Carson-Dellosa

Worksheet 2 (page 65)

Name _____ Date _____

Three-Digit by One-Digit Multiplication with Regrouping

Total Problems:	33
Problems Correct:	_____

Solve each problem. Regroup when necessary.

Hooray for Math!

1. 124 × 7 = 868	2. 813 × 8 = 6,504	3. 379 × 8 = 3,032	4. 288 × 5 = 1,440	5. 585 × 2 = 1,170	6. 703 × 4 = 2,812
7. 956 × 2 = 1,912	8. 486 × 9 = 4,374	9. 377 × 3 = 1,131	10. 496 × 3 = 1,488	11. 778 × 2 = 1,556	12. 539 × 3 = 1,617
13. 453 × 2 = 906	14. 535 × 6 = 3,210	15. 848 × 5 = 4,240	16. 818 × 3 = 2,454	17. 524 × 6 = 3,144	18. 772 × 5 = 3,860
19. 745 × 3 = 2,235	20. 836 × 2 = 1,672	21. 734 × 2 = 1,468	22. 676 × 5 = 3,380	23. 517 × 7 = 3,619	24. 845 × 3 = 2,535
25. 784 × 4 = 3,136	26. 964 × 3 = 2,892	27. 634 × 4 = 2,536	28. 756 × 3 = 2,268	29. 516 × 6 = 3,096	30. 634 × 2 = 1,268
31. 529 × 8 = 4,232	32. 584 × 4 = 2,336	33. 291 × 2 = 582			

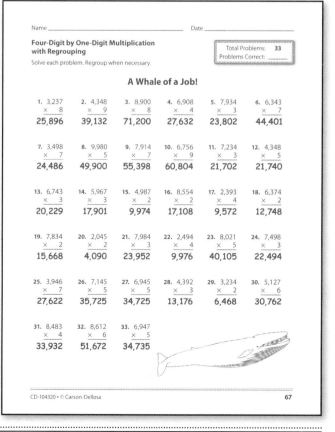

CD-104320 • © Carson-Dellosa   65

Worksheet 3 (page 66)

Name _____ Date _____

Three-Digit by One-Digit Multiplication

Total Problems:	33
Problems Correct:	_____

Solve each problem. Regroup when necessary.

Think Big!

1. 365 × 2 = 730	2. 524 × 6 = 3,144	3. 669 × 8 = 5,352	4. 437 × 6 = 2,622	5. 465 × 2 = 930	6. 594 × 3 = 1,782
7. 608 × 9 = 5,472	8. 548 × 5 = 2,740	9. 623 × 7 = 4,361	10. 589 × 4 = 2,356	11. 336 × 4 = 1,344	12. 121 × 5 = 605
13. 237 × 3 = 711	14. 992 × 9 = 8,928	15. 652 × 5 = 3,260	16. 327 × 6 = 1,962	17. 776 × 7 = 5,432	18. 733 × 3 = 2,199
19. 532 × 6 = 3,192	20. 762 × 5 = 3,810	21. 259 × 3 = 777	22. 476 × 8 = 3,808	23. 649 × 3 = 1,947	24. 324 × 7 = 2,268
25. 122 × 8 = 976	26. 231 × 3 = 693	27. 782 × 6 = 4,692	28. 769 × 5 = 3,845	29. 898 × 5 = 4,490	30. 688 × 2 = 1,376
31. 353 × 5 = 1,765	32. 984 × 6 = 5,904	33. 362 × 7 = 2,534			

66   CD-104320 • © Carson-Dellosa

Worksheet 4 (page 67)

Name _____ Date _____

Four-Digit by One-Digit Multiplication with Regrouping

Total Problems:	33
Problems Correct:	_____

Solve each problem. Regroup when necessary.

A Whale of a Job!

1. 3,237 × 8 = 25,896	2. 4,348 × 9 = 39,132	3. 8,900 × 8 = 71,200	4. 6,908 × 4 = 27,632	5. 7,934 × 3 = 23,802	6. 6,343 × 7 = 44,401
7. 3,498 × 7 = 24,486	8. 9,980 × 5 = 49,900	9. 7,914 × 7 = 55,398	10. 6,756 × 9 = 60,804	11. 7,234 × 3 = 21,702	12. 4,348 × 5 = 21,740
13. 6,743 × 3 = 20,229	14. 5,967 × 3 = 17,901	15. 4,987 × 2 = 9,974	16. 8,554 × 2 = 17,108	17. 2,393 × 4 = 9,572	18. 6,374 × 2 = 12,748
19. 7,834 × 2 = 15,668	20. 2,045 × 2 = 4,090	21. 7,984 × 3 = 23,952	22. 2,494 × 4 = 9,976	23. 8,021 × 5 = 40,105	24. 7,498 × 3 = 22,494
25. 3,946 × 7 = 27,622	26. 7,145 × 5 = 35,725	27. 6,945 × 5 = 34,725	28. 4,392 × 3 = 13,176	29. 3,234 × 2 = 6,468	30. 5,127 × 6 = 30,762
31. 8,483 × 4 = 33,932	32. 8,612 × 6 = 51,672	33. 6,947 × 5 = 34,735			

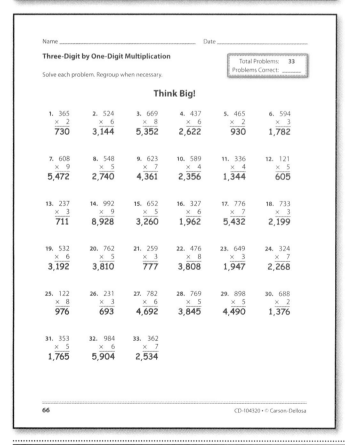

CD-104320 • © Carson-Dellosa   67

Four-Digit by One-Digit Multiplication with Regrouping

Name _____ Date _____

Total Problems: **33**
Problems Correct: _____

Solve each problem. Regroup when necessary.

Let's See Your Smile!

1. 4,113 × 6 = **24,678**	2. 7,312 × 7 = **51,184**	3. 8,900 × 8 = **71,200**	4. 5,308 × 4 = **21,232**	5. 4,930 × 4 = **19,720**	6. 6,342 × 5 = **31,710**
7. 4,213 × 6 = **25,278**	8. 9,980 × 5 = **49,900**	9. 2,794 × 7 = **19,558**	10. 9,755 × 8 = **78,040**	11. 3,214 × 7 = **22,498**	12. 2,317 × 3 = **6,951**
13. 6,746 × 3 = **20,238**	14. 6,677 × 4 = **26,708**	15. 8,227 × 2 = **16,454**	16. 5,857 × 3 = **17,571**	17. 3,351 × 5 = **16,755**	18. 2,356 × 3 = **7,068**
19. 4,845 × 2 = **9,690**	20. 7,934 × 3 = **23,802**	21. 4,065 × 6 = **24,390**	22. 2,132 × 6 = **12,792**	23. 7,021 × 4 = **28,084**	24. 9,442 × 3 = **28,326**
25. 4,365 × 6 = **26,190**	26. 3,225 × 5 = **16,125**	27. 8,222 × 4 = **32,888**	28. 7,422 × 5 = **37,110**	29. 8,265 × 3 = **24,795**	30. 7,120 × 2 = **14,240**
31. 7,322 × 6 = **43,932**	32. 6,434 × 6 = **38,604**	33. 7,387 × 5 = **36,935**			

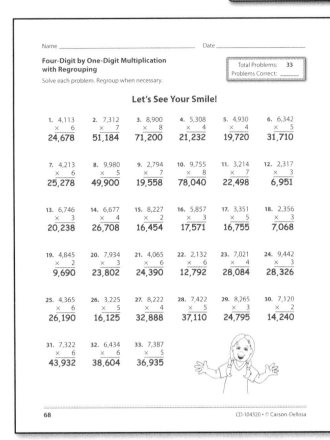

CD-104320 • © Carson-Dellosa

Two-Digit by Two-Digit Multiplication with Regrouping

Name _____ Date _____

Total Problems: **33**
Problems Correct: _____

Solve each problem. Regroup when necessary.

Keep Your Eye on the Ball!

1. 48 × 38 = **1,824**	2. 63 × 73 = **4,599**	3. 67 × 24 = **1,608**	4. 89 × 24 = **2,136**	5. 55 × 63 = **3,465**	6. 39 × 28 = **1,092**
7. 51 × 40 = **2,040**	8. 48 × 69 = **3,312**	9. 58 × 73 = **4,234**	10. 73 × 28 = **2,044**	11. 55 × 33 = **1,815**	12. 88 × 62 = **5,456**
13. 34 × 66 = **2,244**	14. 62 × 44 = **2,728**	15. 68 × 59 = **4,012**	16. 27 × 45 = **1,215**	17. 29 × 89 = **2,581**	18. 53 × 24 = **1,272**
19. 28 × 48 = **1,344**	20. 70 × 47 = **3,290**	21. 50 × 42 = **2,100**	22. 38 × 22 = **836**	23. 45 × 56 = **2,520**	24. 62 × 46 = **2,852**
25. 76 × 49 = **3,724**	26. 66 × 38 = **2,508**	27. 37 × 48 = **1,776**	28. 67 × 49 = **3,283**	29. 67 × 81 = **5,427**	30. 47 × 86 = **4,042**
31. 48 × 29 = **1,392**	32. 45 × 28 = **1,260**	33. 32 × 62 = **1,984**			

Two-Digit by Two-Digit Multiplication with Regrouping

Name _____ Date _____

Total Problems: **27**
Problems Correct: _____

Solve each problem. Regroup when necessary.

See the Fruit of Your Hard Work!

1. 58 × 26 = **1,508**	2. 74 × 49 = **3,626**	3. 69 × 27 = **1,863**	4. 57 × 44 = **2,508**	5. 44 × 37 = **1,628**	6. 28 × 37 = **1,036**
7. 45 × 36 = **1,620**	8. 32 × 49 = **1,568**	9. 59 × 30 = **1,770**	10. 67 × 85 = **5,695**	11. 52 × 47 = **2,444**	12. 54 × 72 = **3,888**
13. 63 × 41 = **2,583**	14. 73 × 55 = **4,015**	15. 36 × 27 = **972**	16. 61 × 72 = **4,392**	17. 37 × 51 = **1,887**	18. 68 × 52 = **3,536**
19. 79 × 22 = **1,738**	20. 48 × 62 = **2,976**	21. 94 × 38 = **3,572**	22. 46 × 79 = **3,634**	23. 67 × 38 = **2,546**	24. 63 × 39 = **2,457**
25. 66 × 29 = **1,914**	26. 51 × 26 = **1,326**	27. 65 × 24 = **1,560**			

CD-104320 • © Carson-Dellosa

Three-Digit by Two-Digit Multiplication with Regrouping

Name _____ Date _____

Total Problems: **27**
Problems Correct: _____

Solve each problem. Regroup when necessary.

Take a Bite Out of Multiplication!

1. 486 × 22 = **10,692**	2. 212 × 56 = **11,872**	3. 333 × 37 = **12,321**	4. 667 × 39 = **26,013**	5. 795 × 48 = **38,160**	6. 583 × 26 = **15,158**
7. 402 × 19 = **7,638**	8. 779 × 31 = **24,149**	9. 376 × 55 = **20,680**	10. 433 × 63 = **27,279**	11. 560 × 35 = **19,600**	12. 731 × 25 = **18,275**
13. 324 × 25 = **8,100**	14. 254 × 87 = **22,098**	15. 107 × 45 = **4,815**	16. 204 × 91 = **18,564**	17. 658 × 87 = **57,246**	18. 547 × 34 = **18,598**
19. 232 × 15 = **3,480**	20. 730 × 32 = **23,360**	21. 477 × 20 = **9,540**	22. 720 × 37 = **26,640**	23. 589 × 27 = **15,903**	24. 526 × 32 = **16,832**
25. 896 × 25 = **22,400**	26. 218 × 13 = **2,834**	27. 539 × 22 = **11,858**			

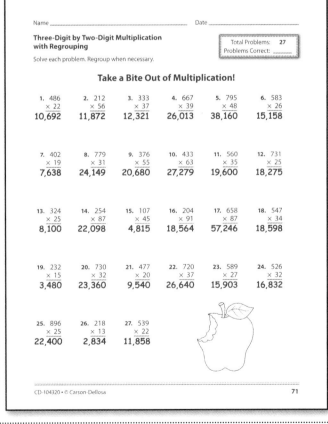

Three-Digit by Two-Digit Multiplication with Regrouping

Name _____ Date _____

Total Problems: 27
Problems Correct: _____

Solve each problem. Regroup when necessary.

Multiplication Is a Hoot!

1. 732 × 28	2. 523 × 84	3. 745 × 22	4. 670 × 54	5. 634 × 99	6. 246 × 51
20,496	43,932	16,390	36,180	62,766	12,546

7. 222 × 37	8. 208 × 40	9. 538 × 88	10. 798 × 55	11. 750 × 58	12. 162 × 32
8,214	8,320	47,344	43,890	43,500	5,184

13. 830 × 65	14. 727 × 42	15. 233 × 28	16. 499 × 21	17. 292 × 68	18. 740 × 45
53,950	30,534	6,524	10,479	19,856	33,300

19. 896 × 35	20. 634 × 32	21. 769 × 42	22. 621 × 44	23. 283 × 30	24. 427 × 40
31,360	20,288	32,298	27,324	8,490	17,080

25. 285 × 46	26. 342 × 33	27. 648 × 32
13,110	11,286	20,736

72

CD-104320 • © Carson-Dellosa

Three-Digit by Three-Digit Multiplication with Regrouping

Name _____ Date _____

Total Problems: 27
Problems Correct: _____

Solve each problem. Regroup when necessary.

Who-oo Likes to Multiply?

1. 325 × 432	2. 265 × 679	3. 721 × 428	4. 236 × 265	5. 123 × 245	6. 248 × 693
140,400	179,935	308,588	62,540	30,135	171,864

7. 343 × 675	8. 649 × 394	9. 476 × 285	10. 438 × 549	11. 845 × 723	12. 722 × 386
231,525	255,706	135,660	240,462	610,935	278,692

13. 434 × 434	14. 365 × 342	15. 362 × 694	16. 998 × 367	17. 554 × 872	18. 351 × 523
188,356	124,830	251,228	366,266	483,088	183,573

19. 569 × 438	20. 460 × 126	21. 659 × 532	22. 448 × 749	23. 538 × 345	24. 477 × 361
249,222	57,960	350,588	335,552	185,610	172,197

25. 258 × 439	26. 453 × 850	27. 241 × 231
113,262	385,050	55,671

CD-104320 • © Carson-Dellosa

73

Multiplication of Decimals

Name _____ Date _____

Total Problems: 33
Problems Correct: _____

Solve each problem. Regroup when necessary.

Thumbs Up for Math!

1. 3.65 × 2	2. 5.24 × 6	3. 6.69 × 8	4. 4.37 × 6	5. 4.65 × 2	6. 5.94 × 3
7.30	31.44	53.52	26.22	9.30	17.82

7. 6.08 × 9	8. 5.48 × 5	9. 6.23 × 7	10. 5.89 × 4	11. 3.36 × 4	12. 1.24 × 5
54.72	27.40	43.61	23.56	13.44	6.20

13. 2.37 × 3	14. 9.92 × 9	15. 6.52 × 5	16. 3.27 × 6	17. 7.76 × 7	18. 7.33 × 3
7.11	89.28	32.60	19.62	54.32	21.99

19. 5.32 × 6	20. 7.62 × 5	21. 2.59 × 3	22. 4.76 × 8	23. 6.49 × 8	24. 3.24 × 7
31.92	38.10	7.77	38.08	51.92	22.68

25. 1.22 × 8	26. 2.31 × 3	27. 7.82 × 6	28. 7.69 × 5	29. 8.98 × 5	30. 6.88 × 2
9.76	6.93	46.92	38.45	44.90	13.76

31. 3.53 × 5	32. 9.84 × 6	33. 3.62 × 7
17.65	59.04	25.34

74

CD-104320 • © Carson-Dellosa

Multiplication of Decimals

Name _____ Date _____

Total Problems: 33
Problems Correct: _____

Solve each problem. Regroup when necessary.

You're Doing Great!

1. 41.13 × 6	2. 73.12 × 7	3. 89.00 × 8	4. 53.08 × 4	5. 49.30 × 4	6. 63.42 × 5
246.78	511.84	712.00	212.32	197.20	317.10

7. 42.13 × 6	8. 99.80 × 5	9. 27.94 × 7	10. 97.55 × 8	11. 32.14 × 7	12. 23.17 × 3
252.78	499.00	195.58	780.40	224.98	69.51

13. 67.43 × 8	14. 66.67 × 4	15. 82.27 × 2	16. 57.72 × 3	17. 63.51 × 5	18. 53.34 × 8
539.44	266.68	164.54	173.16	317.55	426.72

19. 23.23 × 3	20. 48.45 × 2	21. 79.34 × 3	22. 21.32 × 6	23. 70.21 × 4	24. 94.42 × 3
69.69	96.90	238.02	127.92	280.84	283.26

25. 43.65 × 6	26. 32.25 × 5	27. 82.22 × 4	28. 74.22 × 5	29. 82.65 × 3	30. 71.20 × 2
261.90	161.25	328.88	371.10	247.95	142.40

31. 73.22 × 6	32. 64.34 × 6	33. 73.87 × 5
439.32	386.04	369.35

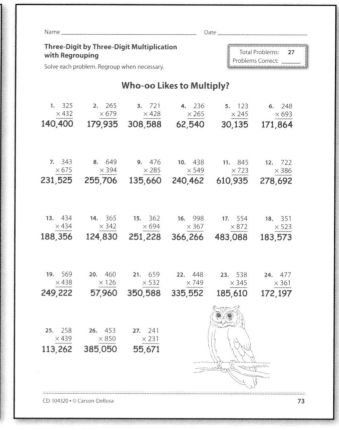

CD-104320 • © Carson-Dellosa

75

Name _____ Date _____

Multiplication of Decimals

Total Problems: **33**
Problems Correct: _____

Solve each problem. Regroup when necessary.

You're Number One!

1. 3.65 × 2 = 7.30	2. 5.24 × 6 = 31.44	3. 6.69 × 8 = 53.52	4. 4.37 × 6 = 26.22	5. 4.65 × 2 = 9.30	6. 5.94 × 3 = 17.82
7. 6.08 × 9 = 54.72	8. 5.48 × 5 = 27.40	9. 6.23 × 7 = 43.61	10. 5.89 × 4 = 23.56	11. 3.36 × 4 = 13.44	12. 1.24 × 5 = 6.20
13. 2.37 × 3 = 7.11	14. 9.92 × 9 = 89.28	15. 6.52 × 5 = 32.60	16. 3.27 × 6 = 19.62	17. 7.76 × 7 = 54.32	18. 7.33 × 3 = 21.99
19. 5.32 × 6 = 31.92	20. 7.62 × 5 = 38.10	21. 2.59 × 3 = 7.77	22. 4.76 × 8 = 38.08	23. 6.49 × 3 = 19.47	24. 3.24 × 7 = 22.68
25. 1.22 × 8 = 9.76	26. 2.31 × 3 = 6.93	27. 7.82 × 6 = 46.92	28. 7.69 × 5 = 38.45	29. 8.98 × 5 = 44.90	30. 6.88 × 2 = 13.76
31. 3.53 × 5 = 17.65	32. 9.84 × 6 = 59.04	33. 3.62 × 7 = 25.34			

Name _____ Date _____

Multiplication of Decimals

Total Problems: **33**
Problems Correct: _____

Solve each problem. Regroup when necessary.

Go for the Gold!

1. 25.72 × 8 = 205.76	2. 33.55 × 6 = 201.30	3. 76.28 × 3 = 228.84	4. 97.65 × 2 = 195.30	5. 67.90 × 3 = 203.70	6. 38.67 × 6 = 232.02
7. 80.07 × 9 = 720.63	8. 82.15 × 7 = 575.05	9. 22.52 × 8 = 180.16	10. 25.86 × 2 = 51.72	11. 76.39 × 2 = 152.78	12. 21.22 × 5 = 106.10
13. 61.56 × 6 = 369.36	14. 73.85 × 9 = 664.65	15. 23.25 × 6 = 139.50	16. 82.52 × 9 = 742.68	17. 20.99 × 8 = 167.92	18. 62.87 × 9 = 565.83
19. 30.59 × 2 = 61.18	20. 61.93 × 6 = 371.58	21. 97.12 × 8 = 776.96	22. 56.19 × 3 = 168.57	23. 58.16 × 3 = 174.48	24. 36.87 × 9 = 331.83
25. 98.20 × 7 = 687.40	26. 29.19 × 8 = 233.52	27. 70.62 × 3 = 211.86	28. 88.38 × 5 = 441.90	29. 35.56 × 2 = 71.12	30. 98.72 × 7 = 691.04
31. 35.62 × 2 = 71.24	32. 27.00 × 7 = 189.00	33. 29.92 × 7 = 209.44			

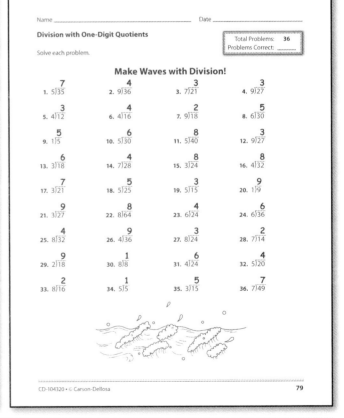

Name _____ Date _____

Division with One-Digit Quotients

Total Problems: **36**
Problems Correct: _____

Solve each problem.

Surf Through Division!

1. 4)36 = 9	2. 5)20 = 4	3. 7)21 = 3	4. 6)24 = 4
5. 7)42 = 6	6. 4)16 = 4	7. 5)35 = 7	8. 3)21 = 7
9. 9)63 = 7	10. 9)45 = 5	11. 8)48 = 6	12. 6)12 = 2
13. 6)42 = 7	14. 7)56 = 8	15. 9)54 = 6	16. 5)35 = 7
17. 6)30 = 5	18. 3)9 = 3	19. 7)63 = 9	20. 8)32 = 4
21. 6)30 = 5	22. 4)28 = 7	23. 9)36 = 4	24. 8)16 = 2
25. 5)45 = 9	26. 4)20 = 5	27. 7)49 = 7	28. 9)36 = 4
29. 8)64 = 8	30. 9)18 = 2	31. 6)48 = 8	32. 6)54 = 9
33. 8)56 = 7	34. 4)32 = 8	35. 3)24 = 8	36. 2)14 = 7

Name _____ Date _____

Division with One-Digit Quotients

Total Problems: **36**
Problems Correct: _____

Solve each problem.

Make Waves with Division!

1. 5)35 = 7	2. 9)36 = 4	3. 7)21 = 3	4. 9)27 = 3
5. 4)12 = 3	6. 4)16 = 4	7. 9)18 = 2	8. 6)30 = 5
9. 1)5 = 5	10. 5)30 = 6	11. 5)40 = 8	12. 9)27 = 3
13. 3)18 = 6	14. 7)28 = 4	15. 3)24 = 8	16. 4)32 = 8
17. 3)21 = 7	18. 5)25 = 5	19. 5)15 = 3	20. 1)9 = 9
21. 3)27 = 9	22. 8)64 = 8	23. 6)24 = 4	24. 6)36 = 6
25. 8)32 = 4	26. 4)36 = 9	27. 8)24 = 3	28. 7)14 = 2
29. 2)18 = 9	30. 8)8 = 1	31. 4)24 = 6	32. 5)20 = 4
33. 8)16 = 2	34. 5)5 = 1	35. 3)15 = 5	36. 7)49 = 7

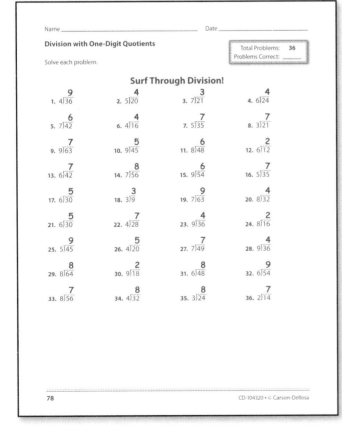

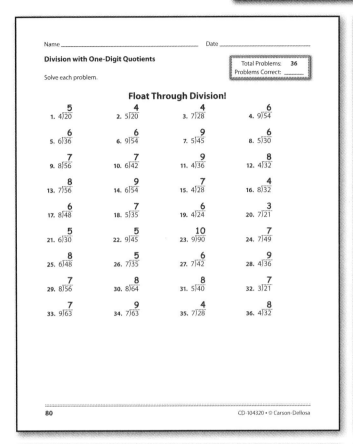

Name _____ Date _____

Division with One-Digit Quotients

Solve each problem.

| Total Problems: | 36 |
| Problems Correct: | _____ |

Float Through Division!

1. 5 — 4)20 2. 4 — 5)20 3. 4 — 7)28 4. 6 — 9)54
5. 6 — 6)36 6. 6 — 9)54 7. 9 — 5)45 8. 6 — 5)30
9. 7 — 8)56 10. 7 — 6)42 11. 9 — 4)36 12. 8 — 4)32
13. 8 — 7)56 14. 9 — 6)54 15. 7 — 4)28 16. 4 — 8)32
17. 6 — 8)48 18. 7 — 5)35 19. 6 — 4)24 20. 3 — 7)21
21. 5 — 6)30 22. 5 — 9)45 23. 10 — 9)90 24. 7 — 7)49
25. 8 — 6)48 26. 5 — 7)35 27. 6 — 7)42 28. 9 — 4)36
29. 7 — 8)56 30. 8 — 8)64 31. 8 — 5)40 32. 7 — 3)21
33. 7 — 9)63 34. 9 — 7)63 35. 4 — 7)28 36. 8 — 4)32

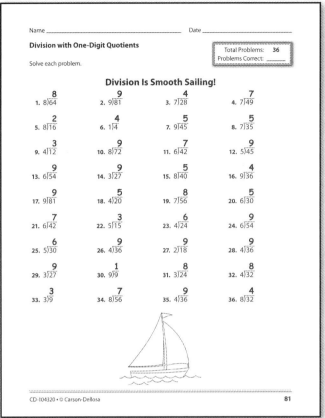

Name _____ Date _____

Division with One-Digit Quotients

Solve each problem.

| Total Problems: | 36 |
| Problems Correct: | _____ |

Division Is Smooth Sailing!

1. 8 — 8)64 2. 9 — 9)81 3. 4 — 7)28 4. 7 — 7)49
5. 2 — 8)16 6. 4 — 1)4 7. 5 — 9)45 8. 5 — 7)35
9. 3 — 4)12 10. 9 — 8)72 11. 7 — 6)42 12. 9 — 5)45
13. 9 — 6)54 14. 9 — 3)27 15. 5 — 8)40 16. 4 — 9)36
17. 9 — 9)81 18. 5 — 4)20 19. 8 — 7)56 20. 5 — 6)30
21. 7 — 6)42 22. 3 — 5)15 23. 6 — 4)24 24. 9 — 6)54
25. 6 — 5)30 26. 9 — 4)36 27. 9 — 2)18 28. 9 — 4)36
29. 9 — 3)27 30. 1 — 9)9 31. 8 — 3)24 32. 8 — 4)32
33. 3 — 3)9 34. 7 — 8)56 35. 9 — 4)36 36. 4 — 8)32

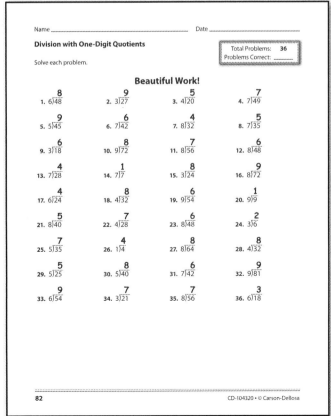

Name _____ Date _____

Division with One-Digit Quotients

Solve each problem.

| Total Problems: | 36 |
| Problems Correct: | _____ |

Beautiful Work!

1. 8 — 6)48 2. 9 — 3)27 3. 5 — 4)20 4. 7 — 7)49
5. 9 — 5)45 6. 6 — 7)42 7. 4 — 8)32 8. 5 — 7)35
9. 6 — 3)18 10. 8 — 9)72 11. 7 — 8)56 12. 6 — 8)48
13. 4 — 7)28 14. 1 — 7)7 15. 8 — 3)24 16. 9 — 8)72
17. 4 — 6)24 18. 8 — 4)32 19. 6 — 9)54 20. 1 — 9)9
21. 5 — 8)40 22. 7 — 4)28 23. 6 — 8)48 24. 2 — 3)6
25. 7 — 5)35 26. 4 — 1)4 27. 8 — 8)64 28. 8 — 4)32
29. 5 — 5)25 30. 8 — 5)40 31. 6 — 7)42 32. 9 — 9)81
33. 9 — 6)54 34. 7 — 3)21 35. 7 — 8)56 36. 3 — 6)18

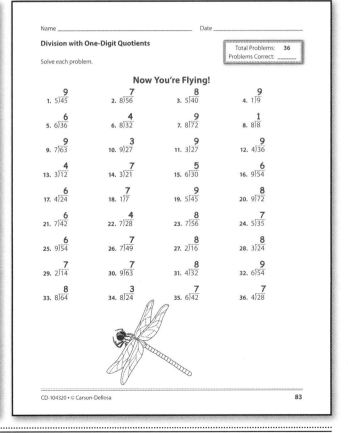

Name _____ Date _____

Division with One-Digit Quotients

Solve each problem.

| Total Problems: | 36 |
| Problems Correct: | _____ |

Now You're Flying!

1. 9 — 5)45 2. 7 — 8)56 3. 8 — 5)40 4. 9 — 1)9
5. 6 — 6)36 6. 4 — 8)32 7. 9 — 8)72 8. 1 — 8)8
9. 9 — 7)63 10. 3 — 9)27 11. 9 — 3)27 12. 9 — 4)36
13. 4 — 3)12 14. 7 — 3)21 15. 5 — 6)30 16. 6 — 9)54
17. 6 — 4)24 18. 7 — 1)7 19. 9 — 5)45 20. 8 — 9)72
21. 6 — 7)42 22. 4 — 7)28 23. 8 — 7)56 24. 7 — 5)35
25. 6 — 9)54 26. 7 — 7)49 27. 8 — 2)16 28. 8 — 3)24
29. 7 — 2)14 30. 7 — 9)63 31. 8 — 4)32 32. 9 — 6)54
33. 8 — 8)64 34. 3 — 8)24 35. 7 — 6)42 36. 7 — 4)28

Name _____ Date _____

Division with One-Digit Quotients and Remainders

Total Problems: **30**
Problems Correct: _____

Solve each problem.

Jump into Division!

1. 4 r5 — 8)37
2. 5 r4 — 6)34
3. 7 r1 — 2)15
4. 5 r2 — 7)37
5. 3 r2 — 7)23
6. 9 r1 — 3)28
7. 5 r2 — 5)27
8. 3 r1 — 9)28
9. 5 r5 — 6)35
10. 7 r1 — 3)22
11. 7 r2 — 4)30
12. 5 r1 — 4)21
13. 4 r8 — 9)44
14. 4 r1 — 5)21
15. 3 r5 — 7)26
16. 4 r2 — 9)38
17. 3 r3 — 8)27
18. 7 r1 — 3)22
19. 2 r1 — 7)15
20. 6 r6 — 7)48
21. 5 r2 — 8)42
22. 8 r1 — 3)25
23. 4 r2 — 8)34
24. 2 r5 — 6)17
25. 9 r2 — 5)47
26. 3 r6 — 7)27
27. 3 r3 — 6)21
28. 3 r5 — 9)32
29. 6 r2 — 4)26
30. 3 r4 — 6)22

Name _____ Date _____

Division with One-Digit Quotients and Remainders

Total Problems: **30**
Problems Correct: _____

Solve each problem.

Hop to It!

1. 5 r2 — 6)32
2. 5 r1 — 8)41
3. 7 r1 — 4)29
4. 9 r1 — 7)64
5. 7 r1 — 8)57
6. 5 r2 — 7)37
7. 7 r2 — 9)65
8. 4 r2 — 7)30
9. 8 r2 — 9)74
10. 7 r2 — 6)44
11. 8 r2 — 6)50
12. 6 r2 — 9)56
13. 6 r4 — 5)34
14. 7 r4 — 7)53
15. 6 r3 — 7)45
16. 1 r3 — 5)8
17. 5 r2 — 9)47
18. 9 r1 — 4)37
19. 4 r2 — 9)38
20. 7 r1 — 5)36
21. 3 r6 — 9)33
22. 6 r1 — 8)49
23. 8 r2 — 5)42
24. 8 r2 — 7)58
25. 9 r1 — 5)46
26. 9 r1 — 8)73
27. 9 r3 — 6)57
28. 5 r5 — 7)40
29. 8 r1 — 8)65
30. 6 r4 — 5)34

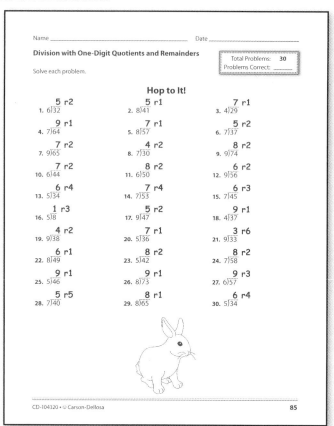

Name _____ Date _____

Division with One-Digit Quotients and Remainders

Total Problems: **30**
Problems Correct: _____

Solve each problem.

Think Big!

1. 7 r2 — 9)65
2. 8 r1 — 2)17
3. 6 r2 — 5)32
4. 8 r2 — 3)26
5. 8 r1 — 8)65
6. 6 r1 — 3)19
7. 5 r4 — 6)34
8. 9 r7 — 8)79
9. 3 r1 — 5)16
10. 8 r1 — 2)17
11. 2 r1 — 2)5
12. 6 r1 — 7)43
13. 8 r1 — 7)57
14. 4 r1 — 5)21
15. 9 r5 — 7)68
16. 9 r3 — 4)39
17. 4 r6 — 8)38
18. 9 r4 — 5)49
19. 8 r3 — 6)51
20. 5 r1 — 8)41
21. 5 r2 — 5)27
22. 3 r1 — 7)22
23. 9 r1 — 8)73
24. 7 r5 — 6)47
25. 5 r4 — 6)34
26. 8 r1 — 3)25
27. 3 r5 — 6)23
28. 4 r1 — 4)17
29. 4 r1 — 5)21
30. 5 r6 — 9)51

Name _____ Date _____

Division with One-Digit Quotients and Remainders

Total Problems: **30**
Problems Correct: _____

Solve each problem.

Sink Your Teeth into Division!

1. 6 r1 — 3)19
2. 6 r6 — 7)48
3. 5 r4 — 5)29
4. 6 r1 — 7)43
5. 3 r2 — 7)23
6. 7 r3 — 4)31
7. 1 r2 — 4)6
8. 5 r4 — 7)39
9. 5 r1 — 5)26
10. 3 r6 — 8)30
11. 6 r3 — 6)39
12. 2 r8 — 9)26
13. 6 r2 — 8)50
14. 5 r2 — 9)47
15. 9 r3 — 8)75
16. 4 r2 — 9)38
17. 3 r1 — 7)22
18. 7 r5 — 6)47
19. 5 r1 — 5)26
20. 6 r4 — 6)34
21. 8 r3 — 6)51
22. 6 r5 — 8)53
23. 5 r4 — 5)29
24. 6 r8 — 9)62
25. 5 r1 — 7)36
26. 7 r1 — 7)36
27. 7 r3 — 9)66
28. 9 r1 — 3)28
29. 4 r6 — 7)34
30. 7 r1 — 3)22

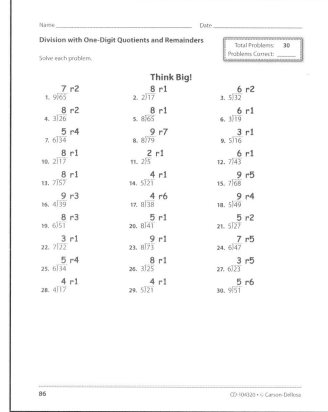

Name _____ **Date** _____

Division with One-Digit Quotients and Remainders

Total Problems: 30
Problems Correct: _____

Solve each problem.

You're Doing an Egg-cellent Job!

1. 8)70 = **8 r6**
2. 4)27 = **6 r3**
3. 2)13 = **6 r1**
4. 3)16 = **5 r1**
5. 6)21 = **3 r3**
6. 5)31 = **6 r1**
7. 9)48 = **5 r3**
8. 7)45 = **6 r3**
9. 8)46 = **5 r6**
10. 9)39 = **4 r3**
11. 6)49 = **8 r1**
12. 8)66 = **8 r2**
13. 9)74 = **8 r2**
14. 6)32 = **5 r2**
15. 2)15 = **7 r1**
16. 3)19 = **6 r1**
17. 7)41 = **5 r6**
18. 5)48 = **9 r3**
19. 5)44 = **8 r4**
20. 7)30 = **4 r2**
21. 9)51 = **5 r6**
22. 4)26 = **6 r2**
23. 6)43 = **7 r1**
24. 9)77 = **8 r5**
25. 8)39 = **4 r7**
26. 7)60 = **8 r4**
27. 4)37 = **8 r5**
28. 7)68 = **9 r5**
29. 3)29 = **9 r2**
30. 4)35 = **8 r3**

Name _____ **Date** _____

Division with Two-Digit Quotients

Total Problems: 36
Problems Correct: _____

Solve each problem.

Get Cracking!

1. 2)84 = **42**
2. 9)99 = **11**
3. 2)24 = **12**
4. 2)46 = **23**
5. 6)66 = **11**
6. 2)66 = **33**
7. 3)69 = **23**
8. 2)62 = **31**
9. 8)88 = **11**
10. 4)84 = **21**
11. 3)33 = **11**
12. 9)90 = **10**
13. 2)68 = **34**
14. 5)50 = **10**
15. 6)60 = **10**
16. 8)88 = **11**
17. 2)64 = **32**
18. 3)93 = **31**
19. 3)63 = **21**
20. 7)77 = **11**
21. 7)70 = **10**
22. 3)96 = **32**
23. 3)69 = **23**
24. 2)86 = **43**
25. 4)48 = **12**
26. 2)68 = **34**
27. 2)26 = **13**
28. 4)48 = **12**
29. 2)84 = **42**
30. 2)66 = **33**
31. 2)22 = **11**
32. 1)11 = **11**
33. 5)55 = **11**
34. 5)50 = **10**
35. 3)39 = **13**
36. 7)77 = **11**

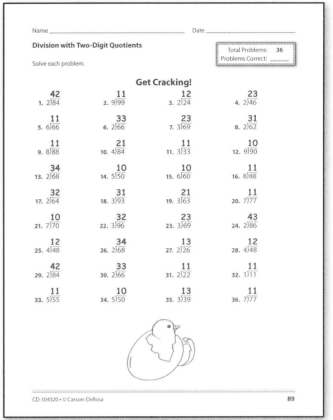

Name _____ **Date** _____

Division with Two-Digit Quotients

Total Problems: 36
Problems Correct: _____

Solve each problem.

Get a Taste of Division!

1. 2)84 = **42**
2. 2)62 = **31**
3. 2)68 = **34**
4. 3)93 = **31**
5. 7)70 = **10**
6. 5)55 = **11**
7. 3)69 = **23**
8. 9)99 = **11**
9. 3)36 = **12**
10. 9)90 = **10**
11. 2)46 = **23**
12. 2)26 = **13**
13. 2)64 = **32**
14. 7)77 = **11**
15. 3)99 = **33**
16. 2)24 = **12**
17. 4)84 = **21**
18. 8)88 = **11**
19. 3)63 = **21**
20. 5)50 = **10**
21. 2)48 = **24**
22. 2)28 = **14**
23. 8)88 = **11**
24. 7)70 = **10**
25. 4)48 = **12**
26. 2)66 = **33**
27. 2)86 = **43**
28. 1)63 = **63**
29. 4)44 = **11**
30. 4)80 = **20**
31. 6)60 = **10**
32. 3)39 = **13**
33. 3)96 = **32**
34. 8)80 = **10**
35. 2)82 = **41**
36. 2)86 = **43**

Name _____ **Date** _____

Division with Two-Digit Quotients

Total Problems: 36
Problems Correct: _____

Solve each problem.

Division Is a Piece of Cake!

1. 7)455 = **65**
2. 3)201 = **67**
3. 7)616 = **88**
4. 3)225 = **75**
5. 8)744 = **93**
6. 5)405 = **81**
7. 6)348 = **58**
8. 4)216 = **54**
9. 6)324 = **54**
10. 2)176 = **88**
11. 5)270 = **54**
12. 7)644 = **92**
13. 2)194 = **97**
14. 6)378 = **63**
15. 2)138 = **69**
16. 3)282 = **94**
17. 9)252 = **28**
18. 8)120 = **15**
19. 8)504 = **63**
20. 9)855 = **95**
21. 3)225 = **75**
22. 9)225 = **25**
23. 3)171 = **57**
24. 3)102 = **34**
25. 4)224 = **56**
26. 5)435 = **87**
27. 4)304 = **76**
28. 5)455 = **91**
29. 2)148 = **74**
30. 7)455 = **65**
31. 9)306 = **34**
32. 6)588 = **98**
33. 2)154 = **77**
34. 7)385 = **55**
35. 4)168 = **42**
36. 8)504 = **63**

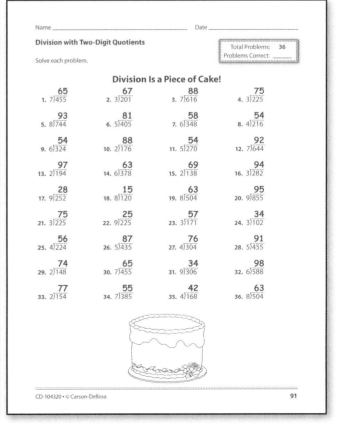

Name _____ Date _____

Division with Two-Digit Quotients and Remainders

Solve each problem.

Total Problems:	36
Problems Correct:	_____

Super Work!

1. 4)65   **16 r1**
2. 7)86   **12 r2**
3. 5)57   **11 r2**
4. 3)55   **18 r1**

5. 2)35   **17 r1**
6. 2)87   **43 r1**
7. 3)74   **24 r2**
8. 6)81   **13 r3**

9. 6)79   **13 r1**
10. 5)93   **18 r3**
11. 4)71   **17 r3**
12. 3)37   **12 r1**

13. 3)95   **31 r2**
14. 3)64   **21 r1**
15. 7)79   **11 r2**
16. 3)68   **22 r2**

17. 8)97   **12 r1**
18. 2)47   **23 r1**
19. 2)65   **32 r1**
20. 2)87   **43 r1**

21. 6)75   **12 r3**
22. 8)97   **12 r1**
23. 5)72   **14 r2**
24. 7)79   **11 r2**

25. 7)95   **13 r4**
26. 4)45   **11 r1**
27. 5)59   **11 r4**
28. 2)53   **26 r1**

29. 2)83   **41 r1**
30. 3)74   **24 r2**
31. 4)53   **13 r1**
32. 3)47   **15 r2**

33. 8)89   **11 r1**
34. 3)86   **28 r2**
35. 4)87   **21 r3**
36. 8)98   **12 r2**

92   CD-104320 • © Carson-Dellosa

Name _____ Date _____

Division with Two-Digit Quotients and Remainders

Solve each problem. Show your work on another sheet of paper. Write your answers here.

Total Problems:	36
Problems Correct:	_____

Jump to It!

1. 8)428   **53 r4**
2. 5)338   **67 r3**
3. 9)479   **53 r2**
4. 4)358   **89 r2**

5. 8)699   **87 r3**
6. 9)245   **27 r2**
7. 9)399   **44 r3**
8. 4)314   **78 r2**

9. 9)758   **84 r2**
10. 8)389   **48 r5**
11. 2)155   **77 r1**
12. 6)175   **29 r1**

13. 3)296   **98 r2**
14. 3)209   **69 r2**
15. 2)119   **59 r1**
16. 5)439   **87 r4**

17. 6)273   **45 r3**
18. 4)345   **86 r1**
19. 7)408   **58 r2**
20. 6)392   **65 r2**

21. 6)237   **39 r3**
22. 8)597   **74 r5**
23. 2)171   **85 r1**
24. 4)231   **57 r3**

25. 5)197   **39 r2**
26. 6)507   **84 r3**
27. 2)137   **68 r1**
28. 7)549   **78 r3**

29. 4)277   **69 r1**
30. 3)173   **57 r2**
31. 7)279   **39 r6**
32. 5)291   **58 r1**

33. 6)319   **53 r1**
34. 5)238   **47 r3**
35. 3)230   **76 r2**
36. 2)173   **86 r1**

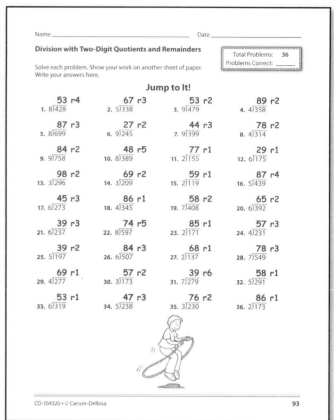

CD-104320 • © Carson-Dellosa   93

Name _____ Date _____

Division with Two-Digit Quotients and Remainders

Solve each problem. Show your work on another sheet of paper. Write your answers here.

Total Problems:	36
Problems Correct:	_____

Division Will Take You Places!

1. 6)537   **89 r3**
2. 7)331   **47 r2**
3. 6)446   **74 r2**
4. 2)135   **67 r1**

5. 8)210   **26 r2**
6. 8)756   **94 r4**
7. 9)291   **32 r3**
8. 5)374   **74 r4**

9. 4)269   **67 r1**
10. 8)307   **38 r3**
11. 3)143   **47 r2**
12. 9)578   **64 r2**

13. 2)157   **78 r1**
14. 9)659   **73 r2**
15. 2)179   **89 r1**
16. 8)532   **66 r4**

17. 5)484   **96 r4**
18. 5)434   **86 r4**
19. 7)439   **62 r5**
20. 9)587   **65 r2**

21. 4)155   **38 r3**
22. 6)562   **93 r4**
23. 7)489   **69 r6**
24. 7)736   **105 r1**

25. 3)119   **39 r2**
26. 2)193   **96 r1**
27. 6)338   **56 r2**
28. 5)484   **96 r4**

29. 8)532   **66 r4**
30. 8)649   **81 r1**
31. 8)757   **94 r5**
32. 3)224   **74 r2**

33. 4)383   **95 r3**
34. 3)143   **47 r2**
35. 4)365   **91 r1**
36. 5)329   **65 r4**

94   CD-104320 • © Carson-Dellosa

Name _____ Date _____

Division with Two-Digit Quotients and Remainders

Solve each problem. Show your work on another sheet of paper. Write your answers here.

Total Problems:	36
Problems Correct:	_____

Take Off with Division!

1. 4)915   **228 r3**
2. 6)652   **108 r4**
3. 2)135   **67 r1**
4. 9)867   **96 r3**

5. 5)238   **47 r3**
6. 9)245   **27 r2**
7. 9)587   **65 r2**
8. 3)224   **74 r2**

9. 8)757   **94 r5**
10. 6)446   **74 r2**
11. 2)157   **78 r1**
12. 2)137   **68 r1**

13. 3)254   **84 r2**
14. 4)383   **95 r3**
15. 5)484   **96 r4**
16. 8)953   **119 r1**

17. 8)389   **48 r5**
18. 9)291   **32 r3**
19. 3)143   **47 r2**
20. 3)119   **39 r2**

21. 5)374   **74 r4**
22. 7)331   **47 r2**
23. 9)758   **84 r2**
24. 3)209   **69 r2**

25. 8)307   **38 r3**
26. 4)269   **67 r1**
27. 8)210   **26 r2**
28. 6)338   **56 r2**

29. 4)314   **78 r2**
30. 7)439   **62 r5**
31. 2)179   **89 r1**
32. 9)659   **73 r2**

33. 2)193   **96 r1**
34. 6)537   **89 r3**
35. 9)479   **53 r2**
36. 6)392   **65 r2**

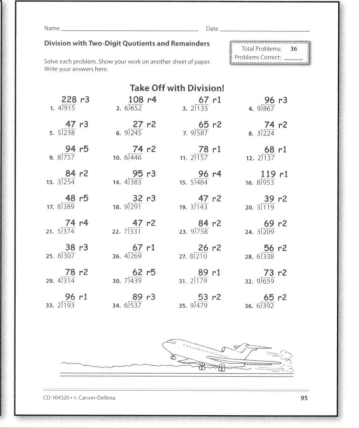

CD-104320 • © Carson-Dellosa   95

Name _____ **Date** _____

Division with Two-Digit Quotients and Remainders

Total Problems: **36**
Problems Correct: _____

Solve each problem. Show your work on another sheet of paper.
Write your answers here.

5, 4, 3, 2, 1...Divide!

1. 4)315 → 78 r3
2. 6)556 → 92 r4
3. 2)135 → 67 r1
4. 9)867 → 96 r3

5. 5)238 → 47 r3
6. 9)245 → 27 r2
7. 9)587 → 65 r2
8. 3)224 → 74 r2

9. 8)757 → 94 r5
10. 6)446 → 74 r2
11. 2)157 → 78 r1
12. 2)137 → 68 r1

13. 2)179 → 89 r1
14. 9)659 → 73 r2
15. 2)193 → 96 r1
16. 6)537 → 89 r3

17. 9)479 → 53 r2
18. 6)392 → 65 r2
19. 3)254 → 84 r2
20. 4)383 → 95 r3

21. 5)484 → 96 r4
22. 8)753 → 94 r1
23. 8)389 → 48 r5
24. 9)291 → 32 r3

25. 3)143 → 47 r2
26. 3)119 → 39 r2
27. 5)374 → 74 r4
28. 7)331 → 47 r2

29. 9)758 → 84 r2
30. 3)209 → 69 r2
31. 8)307 → 38 r3
32. 4)269 → 67 r1

33. 8)210 → 26 r2
34. 6)338 → 56 r2
35. 4)314 → 78 r2
36. 7)439 → 62 r5

CD-104320 • © Carson-Dellosa

Name _____ **Date** _____

Division with Two- and Three-Digit Quotients

Total Problems: **36**
Problems Correct: _____

Solve each problem. Show your work on another sheet of paper.
Write your answers here.

Division Is a Blast!

1. 5)715 → 143
2. 3)942 → 314
3. 3)456 → 152
4. 7)854 → 122

5. 8)896 → 112
6. 3)312 → 104
7. 7)784 → 112
8. 9)999 → 111

9. 4)924 → 231
10. 8)896 → 112
11. 6)726 → 121
12. 7)777 → 111

13. 3)759 → 253
14. 4)856 → 214
15. 5)575 → 115
16. 3)945 → 315

17. 2)432 → 216
18. 6)654 → 109
19. 6)972 → 162
20. 2)548 → 274

21. 4)848 → 212
22. 2)746 → 373
23. 5)715 → 143
24. 4)420 → 105

25. 4)968 → 242
26. 4)932 → 233
27. 5)765 → 153
28. 5)585 → 117

29. 7)749 → 107
30. 9)189 → 21
31. 2)726 → 363
32. 2)952 → 476

33. 7)784 → 112
34. 6)786 → 131
35. 8)872 → 109
36. 7)217 → 31

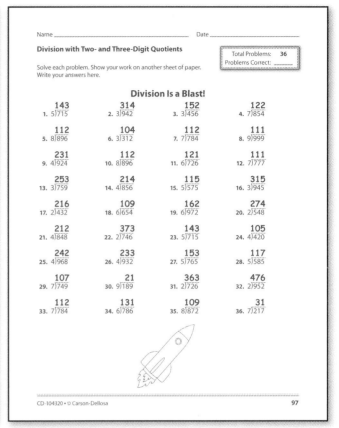

CD-104320 • © Carson-Dellosa

Name _____ **Date** _____

Division with Three-Digit Quotients and Remainders

Total Problems: **36**
Problems Correct: _____

Solve each problem. Show your work on another sheet of paper.
Write your answers here.

Get a Head Start with Division!

1. 7)806 → 115 r1
2. 4)759 → 189 r3
3. 6)887 → 147 r5
4. 7)858 → 122 r4

5. 6)857 → 142 r5
6. 6)676 → 112 r4
7. 3)748 → 249 r1
8. 3)836 → 278 r2

9. 4)635 → 158 r3
10. 8)899 → 112 r3
11. 7)879 → 125 r4
12. 8)978 → 122 r2

13. 5)687 → 137 r2
14. 6)987 → 164 r3
15. 8)907 → 113 r3
16. 4)595 → 148 r3

17. 5)947 → 189 r2
18. 2)337 → 168 r1
19. 2)379 → 189 r1
20. 6)739 → 123 r1

21. 4)675 → 168 r3
22. 2)537 → 268 r1
23. 2)487 → 243 r1
24. 5)684 → 136 r4

25. 3)596 → 198 r2
26. 5)994 → 198 r4
27. 7)858 → 122 r4
28. 6)689 → 114 r5

29. 3)953 → 317 r2
30. 3)647 → 215 r2
31. 2)753 → 376 r1
32. 5)734 → 146 r4

33. 5)748 → 149 r3
34. 5)893 → 178 r3
35. 4)538 → 134 r2
36. 4)629 → 157 r1

CD-104320 • © Carson-Dellosa

Name _____ **Date** _____

Division with Two- and Three-Digit Quotients and Remainders

Total Problems: **36**
Problems Correct: _____

Solve each problem. Show your work on another sheet of paper.
Write your answers here.

Ready, Set, Divide!

1. 4)83 → 20 r3
2. 4)323 → 80 r3
3. 4)842 → 210 r2
4. 6)543 → 90 r3

5. 5)404 → 80 r4
6. 4)283 → 70 r3
7. 5)526 → 105 r1
8. 4)842 → 210 r2

9. 5)453 → 90 r3
10. 7)634 → 90 r4
11. 8)865 → 108 r1
12. 2)421 → 210 r1

13. 8)87 → 10 r7
14. 3)623 → 207 r2
15. 6)364 → 60 r4
16. 3)631 → 210 r1

17. 5)253 → 50 r3
18. 8)726 → 90 r6
19. 6)423 → 70 r3
20. 8)327 → 40 r7

21. 4)483 → 120 r3
22. 9)938 → 104 r2
23. 4)414 → 103 r2
24. 5)517 → 103 r2

25. 2)241 → 120 r1
26. 3)272 → 90 r2
27. 8)839 → 104 r7
28. 7)738 → 105 r3

29. 7)423 → 60 r3
30. 9)98 → 10 r8
31. 7)738 → 105 r3
32. 2)615 → 307 r1

33. 3)92 → 30 r2
34. 6)627 → 104 r3
35. 8)325 → 40 r5
36. 7)426 → 60 r6

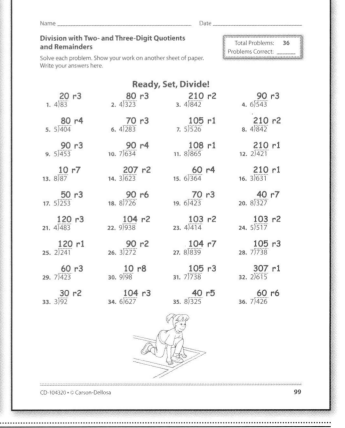

CD-104320 • © Carson-Dellosa

Name _____ Date _____

Division with Two- and Three-Digit Quotients and Remainders

Total Problems: **36**
Problems Correct: _____

Solve each problem. Show your work on another sheet of paper. Write your answers here.

Stir It Up with Division!

1. 3)623 → 207 r2
2. 8)825 → 103 r1
3. 9)98 → 10 r8
4. 5)404 → 80 r4

5. 2)461 → 230 r1
6. 4)414 → 103 r2
7. 5)529 → 105 r4
8. 4)323 → 80 r3

9. 2)615 → 307 r1
10. 8)726 → 90 r6
11. 6)364 → 60 r4
12. 8)865 → 108 r1

13. 4)283 → 70 r3
14. 5)539 → 107 r4
15. 2)841 → 420 r1
16. 3)272 → 90 r2

17. 4)823 → 205 r3
18. 6)627 → 104 r3
19. 2)421 → 210 r1
20. 5)517 → 103 r2

21. 7)426 → 60 r6
22. 3)925 → 308 r1
23. 6)827 → 137 r5
24. 7)423 → 60 r3

25. 7)738 → 105 r3
26. 3)272 → 90 r2
27. 4)842 → 210 r2
28. 5)526 → 105 r1

29. 5)453 → 90 r3
30. 3)623 → 207 r2
31. 6)423 → 70 r3
32. 8)327 → 40 r7

33. 3)961 → 320 r1
34. 5)53 → 10 r3
35. 7)738 → 105 r3
36. 5)253 → 50 r3

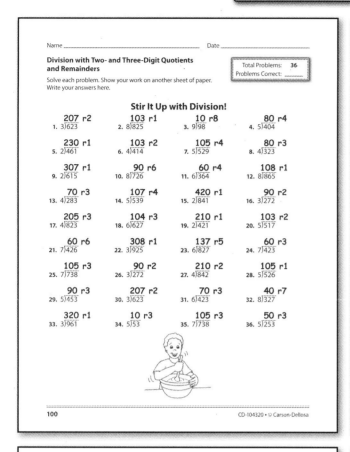

100   CD-104320 • © Carson-Dellosa

Name _____ Date _____

Division with Four-Digit Dividends

Total Problems: **30**
Problems Correct: _____

Solve each problem. Show your work on another sheet of paper. Write your answers here.

Now You're Cooking!

1. 6)7,391 → 1,231 r5
2. 3)2,874 → 958
3. 3)6,238 → 2,079 r1

4. 8)4,376 → 547
5. 6)3,764 → 627 r2
6. 9)2,819 → 313 r2

7. 2)8,497 → 4,248 r1
8. 6)8,149 → 1,358 r1
9. 5)3,381 → 676 r1

10. 4)2,988 → 747
11. 2)8,040 → 4,020
12. 3)3,788 → 1,262 r2

13. 7)5,001 → 714 r3
14. 2)6,841 → 3,420 r1
15. 6)9,469 → 1,578 r1

16. 5)5,328 → 1,065 r3
17. 5)7,384 → 1,476 r4
18. 4)5,978 → 1,494 r2

19. 4)1,538 → 384 r2
20. 2)4,811 → 2,405 r1
21. 7)8,598 → 1,228 r2

22. 4)8,572 → 2,143
23. 3)6,943 → 2,314 r1
24. 6)6,432 → 1,072

25. 8)4,687 → 585 r7
26. 5)5,237 → 1,047 r2
27. 7)4,795 → 685

28. 2)3,486 → 1,743
29. 4)9,035 → 2,258 r3
30. 7)4,001 → 571 r4

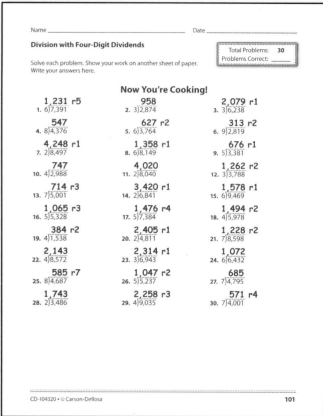

CD-104320 • © Carson-Dellosa   101

Name _____ Date _____

Division with Two-Digit Divisors and Remainders

Total Problems: **36**
Problems Correct: _____

Solve each problem. Show your work on another sheet of paper. Write your answers here.

Stretch Your Brain with Division!

1. 98)99 → 1 r1
2. 40)87 → 2 r7
3. 48)97 → 2 r1
4. 34)74 → 2 r6

5. 21)87 → 4 r3
6. 19)28 → 1 r9
7. 19)88 → 4 r12
8. 37)86 → 2 r12

9. 38)83 → 2 r7
10. 14)73 → 5 r3
11. 19)78 → 4 r2
12. 20)69 → 3 r9

13. 24)82 → 3 r10
14. 25)61 → 2 r11
15. 22)90 → 4 r2
16. 18)61 → 3 r7

17. 22)87 → 3 r21
18. 23)79 → 3 r10
19. 29)93 → 3 r6
20. 23)70 → 3 r1

21. 28)96 → 3 r12
22. 14)85 → 6 r1
23. 18)93 → 5 r3
24. 17)59 → 3 r8

25. 76)94 → 1 r18
26. 35)81 → 2 r11
27. 18)93 → 5 r3
28. 15)84 → 5 r9

29. 21)77 → 3 r14
30. 84)85 → 1 r1
31. 42)93 → 2 r9
32. 12)75 → 6 r3

33. 21)64 → 3 r1
34. 13)96 → 7 r5
35. 77)92 → 1 r15
36. 78)90 → 1 r12

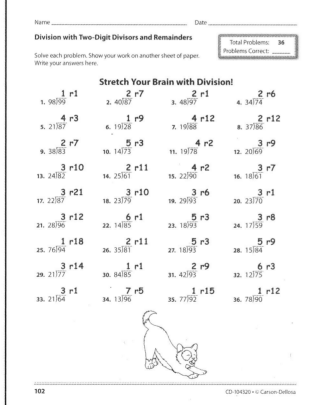

102   CD-104320 • © Carson-Dellosa

Name _____ Date _____

Division with Two-Digit Divisors and Remainders

Total Problems: **36**
Problems Correct: _____

Solve each problem. Show your work on another sheet of paper. Write your answers here.

Math Is the Cat's Meow!

1. 22)419 → 19 r1
2. 18)822 → 45 r12
3. 82)833 → 10 r13
4. 26)375 → 14 r11

5. 38)971 → 25 r21
6. 17)998 → 58 r12
7. 31)563 → 18 r5
8. 68)878 → 12 r62

9. 32)847 → 26 r15
10. 35)819 → 23 r14
11. 67)973 → 14 r35
12. 24)527 → 21 r23

13. 31)827 → 26 r21
14. 77)970 → 12 r46
15. 12)777 → 64 r9
16. 47)822 → 17 r23

17. 88)995 → 11 r27
18. 42)710 → 16 r38
19. 58)902 → 15 r32
20. 94)977 → 10 r37

21. 17)366 → 21 r9
22. 41)886 → 21 r25
23. 43)884 → 20 r24
24. 25)591 → 23 r16

25. 36)915 → 25 r15
26. 57)787 → 13 r46
27. 84)927 → 11 r3
28. 91)952 → 10 r42

29. 34)819 → 24 r3
30. 51)555 → 10 r45
31. 71)977 → 13 r54
32. 46)821 → 17 r39

33. 53)948 → 17 r47
34. 75)888 → 11 r63
35. 19)777 → 40 r17
36. 27)845 → 31 r8

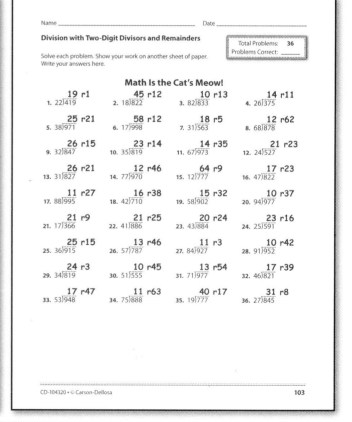

CD-104320 • © Carson-Dellosa   103

Congratulations!

receives this award for

_____

Signed _____

Date _____

$\begin{array}{r} 1 \\ \times\ 1 \\ \hline \end{array}$	$\begin{array}{r} 1 \\ \times\ 2 \\ \hline \end{array}$	$\begin{array}{r} 1 \\ \times\ 3 \\ \hline \end{array}$	$\begin{array}{r} 1 \\ \times\ 4 \\ \hline \end{array}$
© CD	© CD	© CD	© CD
$\begin{array}{r} 1 \\ \times\ 5 \\ \hline \end{array}$	$\begin{array}{r} 1 \\ \times\ 6 \\ \hline \end{array}$	$\begin{array}{r} 1 \\ \times\ 7 \\ \hline \end{array}$	$\begin{array}{r} 1 \\ \times\ 8 \\ \hline \end{array}$
© CD	© CD	© CD	© CD
$\begin{array}{r} 1 \\ \times\ 9 \\ \hline \end{array}$	$\begin{array}{r} 10 \\ \times\ 1 \\ \hline \end{array}$	$\begin{array}{r} 11 \\ \times\ 1 \\ \hline \end{array}$	$\begin{array}{r} 12 \\ \times\ 1 \\ \hline \end{array}$
© CD	© CD	© CD	© CD
$\begin{array}{r} 2 \\ \times\ 2 \\ \hline \end{array}$	$\begin{array}{r} 2 \\ \times\ 3 \\ \hline \end{array}$	$\begin{array}{r} 2 \\ \times\ 4 \\ \hline \end{array}$	$\begin{array}{r} 2 \\ \times\ 5 \\ \hline \end{array}$
© CD	© CD	© CD	© CD

4	3	2	1
8	7	<u>6</u>	5
12	11	10	<u>9</u>
<u>10</u>	8	<u>6</u>	4

2 × 6	2 × 7	2 × 8	2 × 9
10 × 2	11 × 2	12 × 2	3 × 3
3 × 4	3 × 5	3 × 6	3 × 7
3 × 8	3 × 9	10 × 3	11 × 3

18	16	14	12
<u>9</u>	24	22	20
21	18	15	12
33	30	27	24

12 × 3	4 × 4	4 × 5	4 × 6
4 × 7	4 × 8	4 × 9	10 × 4
11 × 4	12 × 4	5 × 5	5 × 6
5 × 7	5 × 8	5 × 9	10 × 5

24	20	16	36
40	36	32	28
30	25	48	44
50	45	40	35

11 × 5	12 × 5	6 × 6	6 × 7
© CD	© CD	© CD	© CD
6 × 8	6 × 9	10 × 6	11 × 6
© CD	© CD	© CD	© CD
12 × 6	7 × 7	7 × 8	7 × 9
© CD	© CD	© CD	© CD
10 × 7	11 × 7	12 × 7	8 × 8
© CD	© CD	© CD	© CD

42	36	60	55
66	60	54	48
63	56	49	72
64	84	77	70

8 × 9	10 × 8	11 × 8	12 × 8
9 × 9	10 × 9	11 × 9	12 × 9
10 × 10	11 × 10	11 × 11	12 × 10
12 × 11	12 × 12	2$\overline{)2}$	3$\overline{)3}$

© CD

96   88   80   72

108   99   90   81

120   121   110   100

⌐   ⌐   144   132

$6\overline{)6}$

$2\overline{)8}$

$4\overline{)8}$

$3\overline{)9}$

$9\overline{)9}$

$2\overline{)10}$

$5\overline{)10}$

$2\overline{)12}$

$3\overline{)12}$

$4\overline{)12}$

$6\overline{)12}$

$12\overline{)12}$

$2\overline{)4}$

$4\overline{)4}$

$5\overline{)5}$

$2\overline{)6}$

1

1

4

2

4

5

3

1

2

2

2

1

3

$\underline{6}$

1

3